The Magnification of the Trinity

The Magnification of the Trinity

To Him All Glory

T. HOOGSTEEN

RESOURCE *Publications* · Eugene, Oregon

THE MAGNIFICATION OF THE TRINITY
To Him All Glory

Copyright © 2025 T. Hoogsteen. All rights reserved. Except for brief quotations in critical publications or reviews, no part of this book may be reproduced in any manner without prior written permission from the publisher. Write: Permissions, Wipf and Stock Publishers, 199 W. 8th Ave., Suite 3, Eugene, OR 97401.

Resource Publications
An Imprint of Wipf and Stock Publishers
199 W. 8th Ave., Suite 3
Eugene, OR 97401

www.wipfandstock.com

PAPERBACK ISBN: 979-8-3852-5036-3
HARDCOVER ISBN: 979-8-3852-5037-0
EBOOK ISBN: 979-8-3852-5038-7
VERSION NUMBER 05/13/25

Scriptures quotations are from the Holy bible, English Standard Version, © 2001 by Crossway Bible, a publishing ministry of Good News Publishers. All rights reserved.

Jessica Bogach
MD MSc FRCSC

For healing

Contents

Prefatory Notes | ix

Introductory Keys | 1

One   Trinitarian Humiliation | 10
Two   Trinitarian Confrontation | 21
Three   Trinitarian Exaltation | 48

Appendix One-Two: Ancient Corruptions | 139
Appendix Two-Two: Contemporary Corruptions | 153
Bibliography | 163

Prefatory Notes

THE TRINITY LIVES. IN the New Testament, he identifies himself as God the Father, God the Son, and God the Holy Spirit.[1] He is the Divinity, active from everlasting to everlasting, incomprehensively eternal.[2] This eternality[3] comprises the Trinity's majestic *base of operation* from which he, magnificent in excellence, governs the created order.

From out of the infinite glories, the coequal and coeternal Three-in-One first magnified glimmers of magnificence at the calling forth of the initial universe, the *very good* universe, Genesis 1:31. To exclamatory praises, Job 38:7, the One-in-Three completed this creative splendor that God the Son commanded into existence.

With the Matthew-Mark-Luke-John Gospel, God the Son supremely revealed God the Father and God the Spirit; through the Incarnation, he *opened* eternity's impenetrable timelessness to make known the Divinity in the decisive glories of the created order.

Now, the grace-infused and post-Pentecost Church, faithful to the Scriptures, still seeks to know the Trinity; reading the Bible, she, maturing, asks the most crucial question, *Who are you?* In every vibrant generation of men and women, young and old, free and oppressed, Asian and African, European and American, or, biblically, Jew and Gentile, God the Son in the name of God the Father and with the ardor of God the Holy Spirit opens

---

1. Since Day One of the first dispensation, the Church knew God the Father as God, and the LORD God, the Son as the LORD, the LORD God, and God, and God the Spirit as the Holy Spirit.

2. Berkhof. *Systematic Theology*, 60, "Eternity in the strict sense of the word is ascribed to that which transcends all temporal limitations." This, as every such definition, fails to penetrate the eternity of eternality.

3. Eternality indicates infinity. Eternity defines the quality or state of this eternality.

hearts and minds to the answer. With this eternal reply, the Trinity omnipotently as well as omnisciently, chronicled the trinitarian revelation for all thereto appointed and confounds throughout all ages idolic, agnostic, or anti-trinitarian obscurities.

TH

Introductory Keys

IN IMMEDIATE POST-PENTECOST CENTURIES, congregational leaders searched the Scriptures to know the Trinity, which knowing builds *the* primary doctrine, the indispensable foundation of the Faith. In the Faith, believing and living, believers recognize inherent tensions within the Three-in-One and the One-in-Three naming; front of mind, they also respect the impossibility to penetrate and disentangle the Trinity.[1] The Divinity lives invisibly from eternity to eternity beyond all ranges of rational and mystical[2] scrutiny.

The Invisible Trinity

In the Faith, believers in post-Pentecost days perceived in Scriptures the invisible God the Father, God the Son, and God the Holy Spirit. Still, the Church, exegeting the Scriptures, acknowledged the Trinity's eternal existence.

---

1. Nicole, Robert, "The Meaning of the Trinity," 1–9, in Toon and Spiceland, eds. *One God in Trinity*, 4, "What is propounded is that there is unity of essence, that this one essence is shared alike by each of the three persons, and the three are conjoined in a total harmony of will and being, which surpasses the unity observed between distinct individuals in humanity."

2. Mystics seek experiential union or direct communion with the Divinity, a trend less taken in rationalistic ages.

Barrett. *Simply Trinity*, 72, according to Enlightenment fakery, ". . . we must look to our religious experience or feeling of absolute dependence on that which is divine."

1

With respect to God the Father's invisibility, sufficing illustrations stand out to recognize and confess this attribute:

> Acts 3:13/Exodus 3:6, to Moses, "I am the God of your father, the God of Abraham, the God of Isaac, and the God of Jacob."
>
> In the grandeurs of eternity, he is the invisible Father to the left of the Lord of hosts, Isaiah 6:1–3.
>
> He is the imperceptible Ancient of Days who addressed the Son of Man, Daniel 7:9.
>
> Matthew 6:18, ". . . your Father who is in secret."
>
> John 1:18, "No one has ever seen God; the only God, who is at the Father's side, he has made him known."
>
> Jesus to a Samaritan woman, John 4:24, "God is spirit, and those who worship him must worship in spirit and truth."
>
> John 5:37b, to a Pharisee grouping, "His voice you have never heard, his form you have never seen."
>
> John 6:46, ". . . not that any one has seen the Father except he who is from God; he has seen the Father."
>
> First Timothy 1:17, "To the King of ages, immortal, invisible, the only God, be honor and glory forever and ever."
>
> First Timothy 6:16a, God the Father ". . . alone has immortality, who dwells in an unapproachable light, whom no one has ever seen, or can see."
>
> He is the One whom Apostle John *saw* seated on the celestial throne, Revelation 4:1–6.
>
> Etc.

Scriptures' Author/authors deliberately attended to the Father's impermeable glory, intently alive far beyond all ranges of rational and mystical acrobatics to access the Trinity.

2

With respect to God the Son's invisibility: distinct from God the Father and God the Spirit, he accentuated his divine agency with preincarnate appearances,[3] summarily:

> He was the One of the *three men* who visited Abraham and Sarah to announce Isaac's birth, Genesis 18:9–15.
>
> He made Sodom and Gomorrah's condemnation happen, Genesis 18:16–21, 19:24.[4]
>
> He wrestled with Jacob. Genesis 32:30p, "For I have seen God face to face, and yet my life has been delivered."
>
> Before him Israel's seventy-four elders ate a fellowship meal, Exodus 24:9–11.
>
> He granted Moses the handwritten Law, Exodus 24:12, 15–18.
>
> He blessed Moses with glimmerings of glory, Exodus 33:17–23.
>
> As the Commander, he invested Joshua with courage to proceed against Jericho, Joshua 5:13–15.
>
> He *permitted* Elijah to see him in passing, 1 Kings 19:9–18.
>
> Daniel *perceived* him as a son of man, Daniel 7:13.
>
> Etc.

For these first-dispensation preincarnate communications, God the Son handpicked men and women to see and experience manifestations of his preincarnate humanity.

Similarly, in the making of the early second dispensation history, as recorded in the New Testament Scriptures, God the Son's invisible divinity shone provocatively in his humanity. In working, by teaching, and throughout Israel's paining rejection, none perceived Jesus' Godness, except through his wise instructions and miraculous interventions.

---

3. Appearing to Adam and Eve upon the Fall, he only spoke; neither of the two saw him, Genesis 3:8–13.

4. "Then the LORD rained on Sodom and Gomorrah sulfur and fire from the LORD out of heaven." The repetitive LORD-naming emphasized that God the Son projected this ruinous destruction upon Sodom and Gomorrah, 2 Peter 2:6, thereby picturing the end result of all sinning communities, however large and strong. Even so Hebrews 10:27.

> Neither Peter, nor James, nor John on the Mount of Transfiguration perceived Jesus' divinity; they saw his momentarily glorified humanity from which they hid respective faces. Matthew 17:1–8; Mark 9:2–13; Luke 9:28–36.
>
> During Jesus' post-Resurrection manifestations, the disciples recognized him in his transformed humanity, Matthew 28:9–10, 16–20; Luke 24:13–35, 36–53; John 20:14–18, 19–23.
>
> Apostle Paul in visions failed even to *picture* Jesus' humanity, its glory blinding, Acts 9:1–9; 2 Corinthians 12:1–10.
>
> And according to Revelation 1:12–16, John *saw* Jesus in his glorified humanity and, Revelation 5:6, also perceived him as the analogical lamb figure, his divinity imperceptible.

Jesus never attempted the impossible: to make his divinity visible. His words and works proved that which even the Twelve were unable to penetrate, the presence of his omnipotence, omniscience and omnipresence. God the Son's splendorous divinity ranged beyond human perception.

3

With respect to God the Spirit's invisibility: from Day One he revealed himself, the vivaciously indiscernible force of life,[5] which characterized his vitality, of which physical graphics:

> On Day One, the Spirit of God hovered over the face of the waters, breathing critical life into the created order that God the Father had devised and God the Son commanded into existence, Genesis 1:2b.
>
> For the progressing-through-the-wilderness Israelites, Nehemiah 9:20, "You gave your good Spirit to instruct them and did not withhold your manna from their mouth and gave them water for their thirst." Did Israel's many ever see the Spirit?
>
> By the Spirit the LORD God enlivened dead-in-sin David. Psalm 51:11, "Cast me not away from your presence, and take not your Holy Spirit from me." And Israel's repentant king lived.
>
> In the cycling seasons, the Spirit provided food for animals. Psalm 104:30, "When you send forth your Spirit, they are

---

5. Owen. *The Holy Spirit*, 29, "He is proposed to us in the Scripture by his properties, works, and operations; by our duty to him, and offences against him."

created, and you renew the face of the ground." In the majesty of providential care, even ocean creatures lived.

Psalm 139:7a reveals the Spirit's omnipresence, the Psalmist asking, "Where shall I go from your Spirit?"

Absence of life typifies death. In contrast, Isaiah 32:14–15, the Spirit seasonally animates the wilderness.

God the Father prophesied life for God the Son. Isaiah 42:1b, "I have put my Spirit upon him; he will bring forth justice to the nations." Matthew 12:18.

God the Son promised Jacob's seed the vigors of faithful living. Isaiah 44:3b, "I will pour my Spirit upon your offspring, and my blessing on your descendants."

The Preincarnate acknowledged boundless pentecostal life. Isaiah 61:1a/Luke 4:18, "The Spirit of the Lord God is upon me, because the Lord has anointed me to bring good news to the poor."

The LORD God carried Ezekiel to Jerusalem. Ezekiel 8:3a, "He put out the form of a hand and took me by a lock of my head, and the Spirit lifted me up between earth and heaven and brought me in visions of God to Jerusalem."

The Holy Spirit breathed life into Israel's skeletal remains that signified death in unfaithfulness. Ezekiel 37:14a, prophetically, "And I will put my Spirit within you, and you shall live, and I will place you in your own land."

The LORD God recalled the Exodus. Haggai 2:5b, "My Spirit remains in your midst. Fear not."

Zechariah 4:6, "This is the word of the LORD to Zerubbabel: "Not by might, nor by power, but by my Spirit, says the LORD of hosts." And, in post-exilic Jerusalem, Israel rooted anew.

At Jesus' baptism, Scriptures present the Spirit as a silently descending dove, Matthew 3:13–15; Mark 1:9–11; Luke 3:21–22.

John 3:8a, "The wind blows where it wishes, and you hear its sound, but you do not know where it comes from or where it goes."

On Pentecost Day, the Spirit fell omnipotently upon the early congregation as a mighty wind and as visible flames of fire, Acts 2:1–4.

And at times, he made himself *visible* to the seven stars, Revelation 3:1. Zechariah 4:10b.

Etc.

All in all, the undetectable Spirit's divinity spellbound the Church through his deliberate works for all thereto chosen to see and believe, John 14:17.

In glorious eternities prior to Day One, the Divinity—without hard boundaries—allocated in the unity of the one will coterminous in creativity, biblically revealed, and thematically recognizable:

> God the Father originated, initiated, gave rise to the creation-idea for the universe.
>
> God the Son commanded the created order into existence, which he since administered providentially.
>
> God the Spirit animated, vivified, motivated, quickened, in short, endowed the created order with edenic beauties of life.[6]

To set artificial boundaries about Trinity-magnifying works misinterprets attributes as well as minimizes the Divinity's magnificence.

---

6. Olson and Hall. *Guides to Theology: The Trinity,* 58, "The functions of the Trinity must be wholly unified so that all three persons are involved in each, but individual persons of the Trinity may be *said to be* especially at work in certain activities of creation, redemption, and sanctification."
Frame. *A History of Western Philosophy and Theology,* 19, ". . . in all aspect of God's work, the three persons are involved. The Son is 'in' the Father and the Father in him. The Spirit is in the Father and the Son, and they are in him. This mutual indwelling is what theologians call *circumcessio* or *perichoresis*."
Poythress. *The Mystery of the Trinity,* 94, "God the Father is preeminently the one who *plans* and *ordains* and *initiates* the course of history and the events that take place. The Father sends the Son into the world to accomplish redemption. The idea of sending presupposes that the Father has already determined a mission for the Son. What the Son accomplishes is what the Father has already planned. The Holy Spirit applies the accomplishments of the Son to those who are united to the Son by faith."
White. *The Forgotten Trinity,* 64, "The Father chose to be the fount and source of the entirety of the work; the Son chose to be the Redeemer and to enter into human flesh as one subject to the Father; and the Spirit chose to be the Sanctifier of the church, the indwelling Testifier of Jesus Christ. Each took different roles of necessity—they could not all take the same role and do the same things." 63, ". . . in eternity past the Father, Son, and Spirit *voluntarily and freely chose the roles they would take in brining about the redemption of God's people.*"
Rhodes. *Christ Before the Manger,* 58, ". . . we must be careful not to make these distinctions absolute."

Now, the Church humbly acknowledges the Trinity's invisibility; in the liveliness of worship and in the hope upon the Parousia,[7] she knows and confesses his presence.[8]

The Visible Church

Within the entirety of the universe, God the Son on a minute planet instituted the Church, from within her to identify his rule over heaven and earth.[9]

Beginning in Abrahamic times,[10] God the Son generated the living Church in the Eastern Mediterranean's Canaan. At the second dispensation's start, he recreated out of the Old Church the New, Christianity her signature.[11] And Christianity, the Religion,[12] perpetuates the continuing Israel, Mark 10:45/Matthew 20:28; John 1:12; Acts 2:39; Romans 4:16–17; Galatians 3:29; Philippians 3:3; etc. With and through the Religion, God the Spirit motivates all joying amplification of trinitarian magnificence.

---

7. Argyle. *Knowing Christianity: God in the New Testament*, 12, "As the keenest incentive of the Old Testament religion was the hope of the nation in regard to the consummation of its history, so the early Christians were from the first spurred on in their moral vigilance and dynamic effort by the eschatological hope of the *parousia*, the final coming of Christ in glory and judgment, which would, they believed, consummate the process of salvation already begun and established by the redemption of the Cross and the victory of the Resurrection."

8. Farrow. "Confessing Christ Coming," 133–48, in Seitz. *Nicene Christianity*, 142–43, "This faith in the *parousia* is a response to the dominical teaching of Mark 13 and parallels, to the united witness of the apostles, and (behind both) to the pervasive testimony of the prophets regarding a decisive confrontation between YHWH and the nations that will usher in an everlasting kingdom—the kingdom of God and of his Christ." This is to say: the Scriptures are eschatologically oriented.

9. Rhodes. *Christ Before the Manger*, 55, "To the naturalistic astronomer, the earth is but one of many planets in our small solar system, all of which are in orbit around the sun. But Planet Earth is nevertheless the center of God's work of salvation in the universe."

10. The earliest identification of the worshiping Church, Genesis 4:26b, died preceding Noah's time.

11. Acts 11:26b, "And in Antioch the disciples were first called Christians."

12. The Religion equals Christianity defined by the Three Forms of Unity, the 1561 Confession of Faith, the 1563 Heidelberg Catechism, and the 1618–19 Canons of Dort. The sixteenth-century Reformation leaders, John Calvin for one, harvested the biblical interpretations of the first five Anno Domino centuries and transformed these teachings in the light of 1) anti-Roman Catholicism and 2) the Scriptures alone, Christ alone, faith alone, grace alone, and glory to God alone.

> The Trinity is One,
> ineffable in exaltation.
> Eternally bonded in love,[13]
> the Three's unicity exists from eternity to eternity,
> infinitely.
> Without beginning and without ending,
> inestimably glorious,
> each of the Divinity magnifies the others.

In the Church nothing else matters, nor in heaven, nor on earth, nor under the earth. Progressive acclamation of the One-in-Three only counts. Therefore, the Three-in-One consecrated the Church to lead the entire universe in glorifying the Trinity. With this exacting goal—glory to God the Father, glory to God the Son, and glory to God the Spirit—the Church moves on from generation to generation into the Eschaton.

In the Church's moving history, to make the Trinity known, God the Son bonded with humanity. Encapsulating the Matthew-Mark-Luke-John Gospel, 1 John 1:1–3a,

> That which was from the beginning, which we have heard, which we have seen with our eyes, which we looked upon and have touched with our hands, concerning the word of life—the life was made manifest, and we have seen it, and testify to it and proclaim to you the eternal life, which was with the Father and was made manifest to us . . .

God the Son through renowned works revealed the Trinity's existence glorious in omnipotence, omniscience, and omnipresence.[14]

True to God the Son, the Church heartily confesses the Trinity: to discerning hearts, the Divinity *exists* from eternity to eternity. On the evidence of the Scriptures, she believes the Divinity, each of whom is equal in the creative splendors of trinitarian unity. As the Three-of-the-Divinity magnify each other throughout all eternity, God the Son summons the Church to eternal trinitarian praises.

The New Testament Church with the liveliness of the Faith early on acknowledged and confessed the Trinity by way of the universal rules of faith—the Apostles, the Nicene (the Nicaean-Constantinopolitan), and the Athanasian. Yet every living congregation still has cause to raise insistent appeals to know the glorious Trinity. *We believe. Help our unbelief.* Such

---

13. John 17:24.

14. Throughout, these three excellences represent the Divinity's entire complexity of attributes.

humble petitioning from out of the Church's Spirit-moved heart seeks out the Bible's basic teaching in order to actually magnify the Trinity.

Throughout the generations, interpreting the Scriptures in the bosom of the Church unnerves denials of the Trinity,[15] both inhibitive lives of little faith and prohibitive absurdities of religiosity; each such man-made religion feigns truths that interfere with trinitarian sovereignty, tempt the Church off the Way, and oversimplify the Satan's aging delusions. In fact, Scriptures mortify these simplistic and humanistic interpretive patterns that compress the Divinity's magnificence into idolism, agnosticism or, worse, anti-trinitarianism. Hence, stirred by the Bible's liberty-mindedness, the followers of God the Son prayerfully solicit to know and confess the Divinity, plus in the holiness of worship to resist "clarifications"[16] of the basic biblical teaching, specifically now the trinitarian.

---

15. Deism, for instance, and Pantheism (all is in God), as well as Panentheism (God is in all).

16. This, by way of two Appendices, involves thinkers as Origen, Barth, Rahner, Pannenberg, Zizioulas; etc.

One

TRINITARIAN HUMILIATION

The Trinity *exists in* transcendent iridescence, divinely omnipresent. Within that omnipresence, he omnipotently and omnisciently created a beauteous universe totally distinct from his infinity. Without making this universe part of himself, in a pantheistic sense, and without enclosing this universe within himself, in a panentheistic way, he exacted out of nothing[1] a glorious entity to magnify himself.[2]

In the transcendence of eternity and out of the ceaseless embrace of joyous glory, as God the Son recalled, John 17:1–5, the Divinity designed, commanded to come forth, and then animated an external entity with kinetic energy. Hence, within his boundless omnipresence, the Divinity ordered the edenic universe into existence, its one and only thoughtful committal to exalt the Trinity.

CREATIVE GLORIES

Within the limitless perfection of transcendence, the One-in-Three (without publishing a humanly accessible manual) elected to summon forth the

---

1. Hebrews 11:3, "By faith we understand that the universe was created by the word of God, so that what is seen was not made out of things that are visible."

2. To ask *why* the Trinity created the universe enters into sacrilegious space. To ask *for what* he created the universe opens up the Scriptures.

enormous created order, its stupendous galaxies uncountable, the whole exultant in rare splendors. Of the Trinity, God the Son spoke the creative commands for magnifying the Divinity.

Creative Words

From out of the eternally joyous, exalting, and perfect trinitarian intra-communion, God the Son effortlessly ordered the non-existent universe to appear obediently in his presence, the whole forever his Kingdom.

1

To start off Day One, God the Son, ruling with God the Father and God the Spirit in the excellences of omnipresence, omniscience, and omnipresence, exhorted his rule into existence. Scriptures verify and clarify the voice of his divine authority:

> Genesis 1:3, "And God said, 'Let there be light,' and there was light."
>
> Genesis 1:6, "And God said, 'Let there be an expanse in the midst of the waters.'"
>
> Genesis 1:9, "And God said, 'Let the waters under the heavens be gathered together into one place, and let the dry land appear.'"
>
> Genesis 1:11, "And God said, 'Let the earth sprout vegetation, plants yielding seed, and fruit trees bearing fruit in which is their seed, each according to its kind, on the earth.'"
>
> Genesis 1:14, "And God said, 'Let there be lights in the expanse of the heavens to separate the day from the night.'"
>
> Genesis 1:20, "And God said, 'Let the waters swarm with swarms of living creatures, and let birds fly above the earth across the expanse of the heavens.'"
>
> Genesis 1:24, "And God said, 'Let the earth bring forth living creatures according to their kinds—livestock and creeping things and beasts of the earth according to their kinds.'"

Through the creative day-by-day account, God the Son commanded the entire cosmos into existence, the whole enveloped in universal splendors, which God the Spirit animated with cumulative intensities of life, Genesis

1:2. From Day One, the free and impressive universe acclaimed the glory of the Trinity.

Trinitarian revelation began immediately in the Day One glory with the *Elohim*-naming, Genesis 1:1; this plural noun with its singular verb demonstrated sources of trinitarian plurality. Further, various exhortations—"Let us . . ." of Genesis 1:26, along with the Spirit's working referenced in Genesis 1:2, plus the "one of us" in Genesis 3:22, the "let us . . ." of Genesis 11:7, and the impactful "for us" of Isaiah 6:8—reveal original evidence for the Trinity's existence, at least a plurality within the Divinity's unity. The creating God the Son, bidding the universe to come forth, simultaneously affirmed the total involvement of the originating God the Father as well as the vivifying God the Spirit, the co-eternal One-in-Three working from within trinitarian unicity.

In the six-day ordering of created reality, God the Son with God the Father and by God the Spirit crowned all creative workings by assembling two creatives. Genesis 1:26–27,

> Then God said, "Let us make man in our image, after our likeness. And let them have dominion over the fish of the sea and over the birds of the heavens and over the livestock and over all the earth and over every creeping thing that creeps on the earth."
>
> So God created man in his own image,
> in the image of God he created him;
> male and female he created them.

Significantly, at creating the initial members of humanity, as distinguished from variegated animality, the LORD God worked alone; on Day Six, Genesis 1:27, 2:7, ". . . the LORD God formed the man of dust from the ground and breathed into his nostrils the breath of life, and the man became a living creature." With this singular creativity he also fashioned the female member. Genesis 2:22, ". . . the rib that the LORD God had taken from the man he made into a woman and brought her to the man." These two adults—meticulously, of one blood!—the LORD instructed to populate the earth, Genesis 1:28, with all eternity to accomplish the command.

These intricate assemblages of the primary human beings gave him most intimate knowledge of anthropological physicality, mentality, and emotionality. Also, most expertly, by creating Adam and Eve with the capacity to believe and will to obey,[3] he grounded both in the Faith, unceasingly to believe and live the magnification of the Trinity.

---

3. Di Noia, "By Whom All Things Were Made," 67–73, in Seitz. *Nicene Christianity*, 69, "Created in God's image, human beings assume a place of stewardship and dominion in the physical universe."

Preeminently, then, the Trinity through God the Son blessed the *very good* universe centered in Eden and on two human beings. In the gloried workings manifested in the purity of the Genesis 1:1—2:4, God the Son confirmed the Trinity's invisible existence, neither his divinity nor that of the Father and the Spirit ever visible.

2

Scriptures repetitively confirm God the Son's priority in creating the Kingdom,[4] work liberally recorded:

> Yours, O LORD, is the greatness and the power and the glory
> and the victory and the majesty,
> for all that is in the heavens and in the earth is yours.
> First Chronicles 29:11a

> The earth is the LORD's and the fullness thereof,
> the world and those who dwell therein, he has founded it upon the sea
> and established it upon the waters.
> Psalm 24:1–2

> By the word of the LORD the heavens were made,
> and by the breath of his mouth all their host.
> For he spoke, and it came to be;
> he commanded, and it stood firm.
> Psalm 33:6, 9

> The heavens are yours; the earth also is yours;
> the world and all that is in it,
> you have founded them.
> Psalm 89:11

> The LORD [formed wisdom] at the beginning of his work,
> the first of his acts of old.[5]

---

4. White. *The Forgotten Trinity*, 32–33, "It was truly novel, in the days when polytheism reigned supreme as the religious 'consensus' of the world, for any to claim that *their* God was the Creator of all things."

5. In times of rising idolatrous belligerency, God the Son claimed the creative wisdom and removed from idols' covetousness any rights to the origins of the universe.

Speaking in the first person singular, personified wisdom originated at the opening up of the created order, Proverbs 8:22–31. The Creator God concentrated on this attribute when he commanded forth the entire fabric of the universe; by wisdom, then, he shaped the totality of his glorious amphitheater in which to magnify all trinitarian perfections.

Wisdom, by more or less following the Genesis 1:1–27 structure, revealed the range of God the Son's omniscience; God the Son took this wisdom-attribute from out of time everlasting—before the waters covered the planet, the mountains and hills contoured

> Ages ago I was set up,
> at the first,
> before the beginning of the earth.[6]
> Proverbs 8:22–23

> Have you not known? Have you not heard?
> The LORD is the everlasting God,
> the Creator of the ends of the earth.[7]
> Isaiah 40:28a

> All things were made through him,
> and without him was not anything made that was made.
> John 1:3

> The God who made the world and everything in it,
> being Lord of heaven and earth,
> does not live in temples made by man.
> Acts 17:24; Revelation 21:22

> . . . yet for us there is one God, the Father,
> from whom are all things and for whom we exist,
> and one Lord, Jesus Christ,
> through whom are all things and through whom we exist.[8]
> First Corinthians 8:6

---

the earth's surface—and delighted in this master architect. Therefore God the Father recognized God the Son the source of wisdom, 1 Corinthians 1:30.

Smart interpretation of Proverbs 8:22–31 now declares 1) that the Creator God ordered the cosmos into existence not out of covetousness, for no man-made gods thrived yet in reprobate imaginations and 2) no idolatrous power projections claimed possession of the universe, not even of the earth. With the magnificence of omniscience, God the Son called on wisdom, one of his excellences, to make all things, ". . . and without him was not anything made that was made," John 1:3.

6. The LORD God prepared his universal creation by making wisdom that excellence with which he executed the entirety of the created order; this wisdom radically excluded covetousness. The trinitarian will to create revealed total holiness, or total sinlessness. Proverbs 3:19 supports the holiness of the Genesis 1:1—2:4 creation.

7. Also Psalms 95:6–7, 96:5, 119:90, 124:8, 146:6 and Isaiah 37:16, 42:5, 44:24, 45:12, 45:18, 48:13, 51:13b, 51:16; Jeremiah 10:11–12; etc., which reveal God the Son's creating word to humiliate overbearing pantheons.

White. *The Forgotten Trinity*, 33, "God often had to remind His people Israel of the most basic of His truths. They were always wandering off into idolatry, attempting to join His worship with the worship of other deities."

8. By naming the Father, the Apostle thereby revealed his originating work; he, in fact, planned the created order, while God the Son summoned the universe into existence. Hebrews 2:10. Rhodes. *Christ Before the Manger*, 61, ". . . creation is 'for' Christ in the sense that he is the end for which all things exist, the goal toward whom all things were intended to move." Romans 10:4.

He is the image[9] of the invisible God,
the first born of all creation.
For by him all things were created,
in heaven and on earth,
visible and invisible,
whether thrones or dominions or rulers or authorities—
all things were created through him and for him.
Colossians 1:15–16

He is the radiance of the glory of God
and the exact imprint of his nature,
and he upholds the universe by the word of his power.[10]
Hebrews 1:3

God the Father to God the Son:
"You, Lord, laid the foundations of the earth in the beginning,
and the heavens are the work of your hands."[11]
Hebrews 1:10/Psalm 102:25–27

Throughout the Scriptures, God the Son, majestically, from out of the trinitarian communion, called forth, Revelation 3:14, "the beginning of God's creation," all that exists, the entirety his exulting Kingdom.

3

Apostles after spelling out the Word's creatorship, revealed from within the trinitarian communion God the Father's originating creativity.

For God who said,
"Let light shine out of darkness,"
has shone in our hearts to give the light of the knowledge of
the glory of God
in the face of Jesus Christ.[12]
Second Corinthians 4:6

9. God the Son's imagebearing pertain to his humanity.

10. Not only is the Son the primary Creator; providentially, he also maintains the created order in its place. Colossians 1:17, ". . . in him all things hold together." Hebrews 1:3.

11. White. *The Forgotten Trinity*, 105, "There is no greater proof of deity than to be the Creator. . . God constantly upbraided the idols of the people of Israel for the very reason that they could not claim to have created the world (Jeremiah 10:10–11). A god who is not the Creator is not worthy of our worship and adoration."

12. Since "Let light shine out of darkness," is at best a questionable paraphrase of Genesis 1:3, actually God the Father's glorious light reflected from the face of Jesus Christ as the knowledge of this glory.

> Worthy are you, our Lord and God,
> to receive glory and honor and power,
> for you created all things,
> and *by your will* they existed and were created.
> Revelation 4:11 (italics for emphasis)

As in 1 Corinthians 8:6, this glorying in God the Father's omnipotent and omniscient willpower stemmed from the manner in which he planned, or blueprinted, the created order, which God the Son then supremely summoned into its radiant culmination. So, consistently, throughout the Scriptures with compounding *it-is-written* impact, the biblical Author/authors revealed, from within the trinitarian bond, God the Son the omnipotent and omniscient Creator. Everywhere in the Scriptures, God, the LORD God, the high and exalted God the Son, transcendent, creatively intensified the glory of the Divinity.

Creative Works

Within the gloriously enormous and hospitable universe, the Creator God concentrated on a single planet harmonic in splendor and kinetic in vitality; the whole earth, even as the universe, glowed with pristine grandeur, matchless in biophysical goodness and peerless with blossoming brilliance, all animal life fearlessly subservient to the first people.

Central to the earth, in Eden, the LORD God created man, male and female. Attentive to crowning the creation, he made both imagebearers and the man officebearer; imagebearing and officebearing aligned the two basic liberties, therewith to represent the creating God. The man initiated his imagebearing and officebearing by naming the animals, which ruling procedure *made* God the Son aware of Adam's aloneness. The man needed a helper to achieve dominion over the earth. Hence, God created the first female of the human race to assist the man in his impressive imagebearing and officebearing, the two straightaway totally committed to this stewardship.

In the midst of the serenity awash in edenic beauty, the Creator God planted two trees, the tree of life and the tree of the knowledge of good and evil, Genesis 2:17; as long as groundbreaking Adam and Eve stayed away from the latter, they honored the goodness of creation, glorifying the Creator God.

In the timeframe of the creating activity and by the initiation of historical movement, the LORD God commanded[13] Adam and Eve to begin

---

13. The Hebrew imperative functions as a blessing formula, with Genesis 1:28 in mind.

populating the earth, thus to vivify rulership. The Creator God willed a peopled planet, to lead his universal Kingdom in voicing its deepest longings, creation's coherent unfolding to magnify the Trinity.

HUMILIATING RUINS

Eve and Adam failed miserably, Genesis 3:1-7. Both ate forbidden fruit. Therewith they shamed the Creator God as well as the others of the Trinity. The two inexcusably corrupted themselves, Eden, the earth, and the created order.

The shock of the Fall reverberated far, ruining the *very good* universe. They, the crown of creation, and Adam the head of the human race, submitted to serpentine covetousness, thereby spreading ruination in the round, universally. The eventual aftermath of the Fall caught the increasing human race in blanket condemnation. Genesis 6:7, "So the LORD said, 'I will blot out man whom I have created from the face of the land, man and animals and creeping things and birds of the heavens, for I am sorry that I have made them.'" From the inflection point of ill-choosing, Eve and Adam's lack of good judgment despoiled the Trinity's magnificent work.

On Day Seven, as the echoes of the LORD's Genesis 1:26-27 exposition[14] faded away, Eve and Adam by sinning toxified the created order. This plunge from the splendorous lights of Genesis 1:1—2:4 into the darkness of Genesis 3:1-7 shocks, its inner brokenness palpable. The two had degraded the exulting *very good* creation; in effect, perilously, they cancelled the future of the Kingdom, the entire created entity sliding away into nullity, the ashes of cremation.[15] In the mortal eruption of sinning, the Serpent had inveigled the two into existential chains of covetousness. They singlehandedly twisted the created order from magnifying the Trinity into *glorifying* an arrogating counter-god who intended by internal disorders to extinguish the astute handiwork of the Creator God.

Abruptly, the command to populate the earth fell away and overcrowding in population centers regulated living conditions. Simultaneous warring over food, water, and land crumpled communal coexistence, communities jealous of essential goods. Peace walked out the door and disharmony

---

14. In Day Seven's context, Genesis 2:4-25 is God the Son's exposition of Genesis 1:26-27 rather than a second creation account.

15. Hebrews 10:26-31; 2 Peter 3:11-12, "Since all these things are thus to be dissolved, what sort of people ought you to be in lives of holiness and godliness, waiting for and hastening the coming of the day of God, because of which the heavens will be set on fire and dissolved, and the heavenly bodies will melt as they burn!"

walked into the centers of humanity. This is to say, magnification of the Trinity disintegrated.

Throughout the first dispensation, the Christ confronted the increasingly malicious idolatries—the fierce spirits of guileful Eastern Mediterranean Baalism, fierce Assyrian and Babylonian pantheons, tolerating Persian Zoroastrianism, and implacable Greco-Roman gods—each determined to *bury* the Kingdom/Recreation under mounds of hatred. At the beginning of the second dispensation, Apostle Paul identified these entombing depths of Adam's Fall, Romans 1:18–32. Romans 1:21–23,

> For although they knew God, they did not honor him as God or give thanks to him, but they became futile in their thinking, and their foolish hearts were darkened. Claiming to be wise, they became fools, and exchanged the glory of the immortal God for images resembling man and birds and animals and creeping things.

Thus the Apostle revealed this divine wrath on the human race, also bared in Romans 3:10–18, that inescapable burden weighing down every man and woman. Grace only removes this colossal heaviness.

RECREATIVE HOPES

The Serpent's invasive hatred and premeditated deception encased the created order within the Adamic ruins of covetousness. Then, intentionally, God the Son—supported by God the Father and God the Spirit—reasserted his universal rule. Out of grace, he initiated the recreation of the Kingdom; simultaneously, he constituted this the Recreation.[16]

The LORD God, before he clothed Adam and Eve to symbolize the cleansing of guilt earned in the original sinning, Genesis 3:21, created another garden. In this other garden, he severely limited the Serpent's covetousness and granted the first human beings the place on earth in which to restart the magnification task. Hence, Genesis 3:14–19,

> The LORD God said to the serpent,
> "Because you have done this,
> cursed are you above all livestock and above all beasts of the
> field;

---

16. With the Kingdom/Recreation's restructuring, the first represents governmental rule, the second *parousiac* beauty.
Farrow, "Confessing Christ Coming," 133–48, in Seitz. *Nicene Christianity,* 144, "The church's concern is, as far as possible, to put the world on notice of the question (about the coming of the Parousia), and to show Jew and Gentile alike that the proper answer can be given and false answer avoided."

> on your belly you shall go,
> and dust you shall eat all the days of your life.
> I will put enmity between you and the woman,
> and between your offspring and her offspring;
> he shall bruise your head,
> and you shall bruise his heel."
> To the woman he said,
> "I will surely multiply your pain in childbearing;
> in pain you shall bring forth children.
> Your desire shall be for your husband,
> and he shall rule over you."[17]
> And to Adam he said,
> "Because you have listened to the voice of your wife
> and have eaten of the tree of which commanded you,
> 'You shall not eat of it,
> cursed is the ground because of you;
> in pain you shall eat of it all the days of your life;
> thorns and thistles it shall bring forth for you;
> and you shall eat the plants of the field.
> By the sweat of your face you shall eat bread,
> till you return to the ground,
> for out of it you were taken;
> for you are dust,
> and to dust you shall return."

Against damaging malignities of hatred and unruly desires of covetousness, the LORD God actuated the second universe, beginning with a weed-infested garden, its initial beauty the hope of the Incarnation. Thus unilateral re-rooting of the Kingdom/Recreation started the millennia-long confrontation recorded throughout the Old Testament Scriptures. The LORD constructed this history on one level as the Serpent's fated off-ramp into total perdition and on another this history matured into the Christ's regeneration of his rule, Matthew 19:28. The lengthy biblical record—the LORD God with the Incarnation breaking the created order free from its Adamic ruination—indicates the tremendous impact of the original sin.

---

17. At restructuring the Adam-Eve marital bond, the LORD God renewed Eve's helper status of Genesis 2:20. He never opened a door into misogynistic hatred. In fact, he with the most direct language restored Eve to helping Adam in his headship.

First Summation

With the Genesis 3:14–19 eschatological anticipation alive in the first dispensation, God the Son from out of his trinitarian majesty numerous times seized the initiative, prolonging the long war 1) for the sake of shepherding every last one of the elect into the Church, 2) for bringing about the fiery end of the entire satanic hegemony, and 3) for recreating the supreme magnification of the Trinity, signal victories that built covenant commitment.

Two

TRINITARIAN CONFRONTATION

FROM DAY ONE, GOD the Son, the creating God of Genesis 1:1—2:3 and the expositing God of Genesis 2:4–25, manifested himself as the Divinity's public voice. He ordered all created reality into existence and interpreted the meaning of its enormous entirety, down to the two creatives, Adam and Eve. As the commanding Deity, he irresistibly summoned the hitherto nonexistent universe to appear in obedience before him, the human beings illustrative of his omnipotence and omniscience.

By speaking, God the Son opened the first galvanizing look at the Trinity, God the Father and God the Spirit fully collaborative. In unity and in eternity, the Three cooperatively elected to create an awe-inspiring universe as well as a winnable people to praise and glorify him, the Divinity.

Glorification belongs to the nature of the Divinity; as the Father glorifies the Son and the Spirit, as the Son glorifies the Father and the Spirit, so the Spirit glorifies the Father and the Son—without the least degree of hierarchy. In the eternal upwelling of this unity in exaltation, the Three-in-One nevertheless willed an outside holy acclaim.[1] In the perfection of perfections, the like-minded and one-willed Divinity through God the Son revealed the invincible heart of the Trinity, for magnification upon magnification.

---

1. Was the Trinity lonely?
Was the Trinity internally dissatisfied?
Was the Trinity-glory slackening off, in need of an outside boost?

Throughout Genesis 3:8—Malachi 4:6, malevolently, the Serpent with insufferable arrogance sought to arrogate all praise to himself; therefore he strove against trinitarian omnipotence, omniscience, even omnipresence, to enslave Eve's seed, the Seed as well, in which supercilious pretense he failed the grasp the authority of divine authority.

However malevolent the arrogating Serpent, nevertheless, God the Father, God the Son, and God the Spirit pursued the ultimacy of the created order, the Divinity's eternal magnification. To this end, the Trinity with unyielding commitment activated permanently synchronous workings.

The Working Father

Fundamental to creation, God the Father from within the glories of the Divinity laid the groundwork for trinitarian movement. All the while, he remained invisible, his divinity beyond all rational and mystical curiosities. Of this preparatory, *behind-the-scenes,* great-mindedness exemplifying instances:

First, God the Father with respect to the Exodus fully assembled the groundplan for Israel's release from Egyptian slavery, Exodus 3:1—4:17. To convey this plan, the angel of the Lord summoned Moses to attend to the burning bush. Then God the Father from out of fiery glory commanded[2] the man to approach unshod and listen to his deep-rooted sympathy for Israel's predicament. Exodus 3:7-8, "I have surely seen the affliction of my people who are in Egypt and have heard their cry because of their taskmasters. I know their sufferings, and have come down to deliver them out of the hand of the Egyptians and to bring them up out of that land to a good and broad land, a land flowing with milk and honey, to the place of the Canaanites, the Hittites, the Amorites, the Perizzites, the Hivites, and the Jebusites." Foundationally, God the Father, Exodus 3:6/Acts 3:13, marked out the elemental, indeed, lively outline for Israel's liberty.

Second, God the Father from out of his glory explicitly moved, enabled, and commissioned Moses to undertake the leadership for Israel's freedom journeying. Thus the God of Abraham, Isaac, and Jacob, Exodus 3:16, primed Moses and Israel for the Exodus by shunting Egyptian enslavers aside and liberating his covenant people.

---

2. The *how* of God the Father's conversation with a not very communicative Moses intrigues. He irresistibly drove the fractious man in this back-and-forth argumentation to comply. More such divinely initiated communicative ways the Old Testament Scriptures records—conversations, visions, dreams, and prophecies—happen no more; since the completion of the Scriptures, the Bible suffices for all divine communication to the Church.

Pertinently now, God the Father constructed the groundwork for the Exodus, to defeat Egypt and resurrect Israel.

Throughout the first dispensation's prophetic writings, God the Father at times *interrupted* God the Son's foretelling. In Isaiah specifically the Father emboldened the Preincarnate to carry out all salvific workings. For this purpose, the prophetic proclamation alternated not so subtly in pronominal activity, of which different existential instances:

> Behold my servant,[3] whom I uphold,
> my chosen, in whom my soul delights;
> I have put my Spirit upon him;
> he will bring forth justice to the nations.
> He will not cry aloud or lift up his voice,
> or make it heard in the street;
> a bruised he will not break,
> and a faintly burning wick he will not quench;
> he will faithfully bring forth justice.
> He will not grow faint or be discouraged
> till he has established justice in the earth;
> and the coastlands wait for his law.
> Isaiah 42:1–4/Matthew 12:18–21

And again, God the Father definitively and decisively prefigured the ground-plan for the Incarnation.

> Assemble, all of you, and listen!
> Who among [the fake deities] has declared these things?
> The LORD loves him;
> he shall perform his purpose on Babylon,
> and his arm shall be against the Chaldeans.
> I, even I, have spoken and called him;
> I have brought him, and he will prosper in his way.
> Draw near to me, hear this:
> from the beginning I have not spoken in secret,
> from the time it came to be I have been there.
> Isaiah 48:14–16b

By way of these prophetic breaks, God the Father—preparatory to the Incarnation—authoritatively summoned Israelites to reject invasive Assyrian and Babylonian religiosities in order that they hear the LORD God.[4] God the Father speaking from within Old Testament shadows addressed

---

3. Acts 3:13, 4:30; etc., with reference to Jesus' humanity.

4. In other instances, too, comprising Isaiah 49:1–7, 50:4–9, 51:9–11, God the Father interrupted the flow of the Son's prophetic speech.

the Old Church with the Kingdom/Recreation in mind. By way of Isaiah 52:13—53:12[5] God the Father in a most compelling manner commanded Israel to hear the Son. The past tense throughout these chapters asserts that the Gospel is unalterably fixed in the Trinity's eternality.

One more. Micah 5:2 also affirms this pronominal change of voice.

> But you, O Bethlehem Ephrathah,
> who are too little to be among the clans of Judah,
> from you shall come forth for me one who is to be ruler in Israel,
> whose coming forth is from of old,
> from ancient days.

This reference to the Christ's preexistence affirms his eternality, which Habakkuk 1:12 confirmed.

Also, God the Father *appeared* as the Ancient of Days, so recounted in Daniel 7:13, showing concurrently a prescient vision of the Lamb of God, the ascended Son of Man who had condemned mightiest empires and strongest idolatries.[6]

Out of his invisibility, God the Father with all glorious resplendence revealed geopolitical as well as ecclesiastical workings to reconstruct the Kingdom/Recreation, thereby contributing prophetically to magnify the Trinity.

The Working Son

As before Adam's sin, so after the Fall: God the Son from out of the glories of the Divinity structured the history of the first dispensation.[7] He cleansed the earth with the Flood. He eliminated the Plain-of-Shinar grandiosity. He called Abraham. He created the Exodus. He carried Israel to Canaan, Deuteronomy 1:31. He raised up the Davidic monarchy. He forced the Exile. He rebuilt Jerusalem. All the while, he, the God of gods and Lord of lords, compelled reluctant kingdoms and antagonistic empires to give way. As the Preincarnate readying for the Incarnation, he intended with the benefit of foresight to accomplish his omnipotent Genesis 3:14–19 hope.

---

5. Acts 3:18, "... what God foretold by the mouth of all the prophets, that his Christ would suffer, he thus fulfilled."

6. In Revelation 5:6–7, the triumphing divine/human Lamb resumed at God the Father's right hand the government of the Kingdom/Recreation and the universe.

7. Matthew 5:17; Luke 24:27, 44; John 5:39; Hebrews 10:7; etc., reveal the Old Testament's Christocentricity.

1

As God the Son, great, mighty, awesome, upon the Adamic Fall ignited the first dispensation's beacon of hope, the Serpent masterminded many bewildering follies and furies to confound the entire creation. At the Christ's founding of the Kingdom/Recreation, Satan sought with vagrant desperation to enclose the divine dominion within tyrannizing evils. With startling ease he had mutated the entirety of the created order into chronic revolutionary and immoral degeneracies; now, post-Adamic, he willed with similar effortlessness to superimpose his corrosive legacy universally. Through the long and dark night begun on the evening of the Seventh Day, the Serpent with demonic urgency to humiliate God the Son, polarized all reality, he on the dark side.

At gaining Adam, the head of the human race and its earliest officebearer, the Serpent—iniquitous to the core—pressed the first generations of the Kingdom/Recreation into ruination. His consummate goal, readily readable on the Genesis 3:8–6:8 pages, included foremost Cainite proxies bedeviling God the Son to force his submission. The Serpent planned this humiliation by disintegrating the entire creation the LORD had commanded into existence, even if he finally ruled over its cremated remains.

In the fleeting moment of deceiving Adam, the Serpent exhibited the pinnacle of totalitarianism; in that lowest vortex of unsullied evil, he lost; unable to overcome God the Son, the Serpent invented other scandalous means and methods of deceit to *murder* God the Son. Active in rebellion and reckless in disparaging the God of gods, he lured Seth's descendants into Cain's revolutionary counter-culture, except for Noah's Eight.

God the Son, supremely averse to surrendering the Kingdom/Recreation to the covetous violence of mighty men, inundated the earth with the globally immersive Deluge; he cleansed away the Cain/Seth civilization, saving but Eight, 1 Peter 3:20. To these Eight and descendants—Noah the pace-setting imagebearer and officebearer—God the Son entrusted the light and the hope of the Genesis 3:14–19 Kingdom/Recreation, in order to make the Faith happen.[8]

The generations after Noah, Genesis 10:32, committed wholeheartedly to idolatry; they planned a monumental ziggurat[9] to build heights of hostility. Instead of magnifying the God the Son, the Plain-of-Shinar

---

8. Barrett. *Simple Trinity*, 111, "For all our healthy focus on what God has done to save us, we might talk and talk and talk about *our* salvation and forget to talk about the gospel's ultimate object of adoration: the triune God himself."

9. At the very top of such later constructions, priests sacrificed to the then current deity, or deities, to persuade these fantasies to people-pleasing ends.

tower-builders willed the construction of this altar of unity to provide the Serpent with imaginary global ownership. The Plain of Shinar became the original breeding grounds for idolatry; only afterward do the first religiosities appear.

God the Son *swayed* the rebelliously narrow-minded Plain-of-Shinar idolaters to actually populate the earth, per Genesis 1:28, 9:1, 7; he broke the inward-looking dreams of self-glorification and, synchronizing this work with that of God the Father and God the Spirit, sent all wandering away to divinely appointed homelands. Bluntly, he sovereignly dismissed language-challenged, incommunicative masses to far-flung places of belonging and they, grudgingly obedient to the population mandate, globally erected population centers built on idolatrous,[10] that is, sandy foundations, each town and city allegedly protected by little gods and goddesses carried away from the Plain-of-Shinar or invented as the founder(s) of these communities.

From out of those idolatrous communities, peoples with hostile intent fought each other over the wealth of the nations: food, water, and land. This covetous turmoiling turned into the hard evidence that God the Son had assigned each civilization to perpetrate its own reprobation. Those cultures and societies, then, burdened by the Shem-Ham-Japheth religiosities, *freed* the Serpent to fancy effortless control over the earth; by encumbering those pioneers with assortments of gods and goddesses he displayed an outward conformity,[11] even while he quickened racial hatred, ecological destruction, and toxic warring that through the generations retarded world peace.

Hence, by way of proliferating ancestral faiths, the Serpent *owned* centers radiating control; peoples by worshiping his effigies eased elemental loneliness under star-lit skies and fought off constrictive isolation within sun-bright horizons. Yet, the idol-lights of those ancestral faiths darkened the darkness and the idol-hopes of the religiosities complicated the

---

10. Idolatry consists of deifying created things. Deuteronomy 4:16–19/Romans 1:22–23, "Claiming to be wise, they became fools, and exchanged the glory of the immortal God for images resembling mortal man and birds and animals and creeping things." Psalm 106:20. Jeremiah 2:11. Scriptures measure the error of idolization by the fore-planned wrath of God and the punishment Christ Jesus imposes.

Ideology consists of the deification of an idea, an idea as large as the Renaissance-Enlightenment-Modernism-Postmodernism illusion, as perverse as transgenderism, and as broad as idealism itself. When ideas concretize idolatrously, proponents fire up tyranny in its multitudinous modes of hatred. Ideologies form off-ramps into idolatry.

11. Haidt. *The Anxious Generation,* 203, "The strongest and most satisfying communities come into being when something lifts people out of the lower level so that they have powerful collective experiences. They all enter the realm of the sacred together, at the same time. When they return to the profane level, where they need to be most of the time to address the necessities of life, they have greater trust and affection for each other as a result of their time together in the sacred realm."

hopelessness. At *magnifying* the Serpent to guarantee self-preservation, the peoples discovered the new average to which the dying and the dead adjusted.

The Serpent, unable to circumvent or maximally deprecate the LORD's omnipotent, omniscient, and omnipresent authority, in his evolution of evil nevertheless gained limited domination by conflictive creeds, racial hates, and petty claims to imperial ownership. To that end, he splintered his demonic rule over proxies, the easier therewith to simulate the normality of his infernal dominance. Through the process of normalizing idolatry— peoples isolated behind bars of greed and blinded by devastations of self-indulging—the Enemy consolidated his indefensible lines of division.

Out of the Serpent's bilious acclaim for impossible gods and goddesses housed in pantheonic causes of friction, God the Son directed the Semite Abram/Abraham to Canaan, the man's stopping-place and center of life. By freeing this man from indecisive drifting and from forever falling victim to doting religiosities, the LORD God once more made the Serpent suffer defeat, his flaunted rulership in paralysis.

As world populations, overwhelmed in confusions of covetousness, peopled the dark side of the dividing-line, the LORD God called Abram/Abraham, Genesis 12:1-3, forever reputed the father of all believers, Romans 4:1-12; Galatians 3:7-9. In the hour of his calling, the man found Canaan his earthly destination. As he had done to Noah's Eight, the God of heaven and earth now revealed to Abram/Abraham with Sarai/Sarah magnanimities of grace.

Abraham's lineage by Sarah through Isaac and Jacob/Israel knew of Kenite, Kenizzite, Kadmonite, Hittite, Perizzite, Rephaimite, Amorite, Canaanite, Girgashite, and Jebusite religiosities, Genesis 15:19-21. And Israel from out of the freedom of the Faith recognized the intrusive proximity of the Egyptian pantheon, Exodus 1:8-14, also of Canaanite, Hittite, Amorite, Perizzite, Hivite, and Jebusite idolatries, Exodus 3:8, along with Amalekite, Exodus 17:8-13, Edomite, Numbers 20:14-21, Ammonite, Numbers 21:21-26, Moabite, Numbers 22:1-6, Midianite, Judges 6:1-6, Philistine, Judges 13:1, Syrian, 1 Kings 20:1-6, Assyrian, 2 Kings 16:7-9, Babylonian, 2 Kings 20:12-15, Persian, Ezra 1:1, and thereafter Grecian and Roman belligerencies. Those civilizations under imperatives of pantheonic deities stumbled about in darkness and succumbed to perdition, while Abraham's family lived.

The LORD God executed the Exodus, Israel's liberation from submergence in slavery and genocidal death, its Decalogue the way of liberation. This dominant Old Testament historical event magnified God the Son, Exodus 15:11-12; Deuteronomy 6:4. In consequences, the idolizing nations on and surrounding the Eastern Mediterranean land bridge trembled in fear, as God the Son intended.[12] Exodus 15:14–16, 23:27,

> I will send my terror before you and will throw into confusion all the people against whom you shall come, and I will make all your enemies turn their backs to you.

Similarly Joshua 2:8–11.[13] Moreover, after the LORD God devastated the Egyptian pantheon, Exodus 12:12, all contiguous civilizations lost resolve to oppose him and his Israel, unable to drive the elect nation out of existence. In addition to clearing the way ahead by spreading this paralyzing fear, the Exodus served Israel as a propellant through the desert journeying and at transitional points;[14] according to the sacred narrative, the LORD willed this people to magnify him in righteousness.

By continual confrontation, the eclectic faiths against the Faith and the pantheonic deities against the LORD God, he upon the Exodus tested Israel against these default religiosities dominating the Eastern Mediterranean, the Baalisms. Israel, answering, withdrew into this darkness of gods and semi-gods, which permitted the Serpent to assume he spun the covenant people's existential life-choices and mold the Kingdom/Recreation's every tomorrow. When one small Baal-nation, the Philistine, had nearly eliminated Israel, the LORD through Samuel anointed David, son of Jesse, under whom the Kingdom/Recreation reached the borders promised Abram/Abraham, Genesis 15:17–21; 1 Kings 4:21. After him, except for faithful Davidides, the Kingdom/Recreation and, hence, the universe, nearly toppled, sinking into the Serpent's ruination.

Still, the LORD God with holy authority fervently fought on, in the long war confronting the Serpent's proxies. Yet, over the centuries, the citizens of the Kingdom/Recreation surrendered to Assyrian, Babylonian, and Grecian/Roman idolatries. And terribly humiliating for God the Son, for from inside the Religion Pharisaism/Sadduceism assumed rulership; powers most incompatible with the Religion afflicted the Kingdom/Recreation. Once more, the Serpent almost succeeded. In the darkness of Pharisaism/

---

12. See now that I, even I, am he,
    and there is no god beside me;
    I kill and I make alive;
    I wound and I heal;
    and there is none that can deliver out of my hand.
    Deuteronomy 32:39

13. Numbers 22:3; Joshua 3:10, 4:24, etc.

14. As fully functioning signs: Psalms 66:5–7, 77:15–16, 78:11–14, 103:7, 106:6–9, 135:8–12, 136:10–16; Isaiah 51:9–11; Hosea 11:1/Matthew 2:15; etc. The LORD created only Israel the light to the nations, Isaiah 42:6, 49:6.

Sadduceism, God the Son at the Incarnation entered into the Kingdom/Recreation for the reformation of the Religion, to summon forth out of a perishing Israel a remnant for his everlasting dominion.

The Serpent/Devil/Satan's indelicate persistence to demolish God the Son by savaging the Kingdom/Recreation with hegemonic evil reached its depths of degeneracy and desperation: either he enter into the hell of everlasting fire or rule over the utterly ruined Kingdom/Recreation. At the end of the long war and the long night of demonic tyranny, a characteristic of the Old Testament history, the overpowering Light of the world shone in the darkness, John 1:5.

2

Throughout the Old Testament millennia, the LORD God in display of his divinity owned evocative names, each expressive of his excellence—*El, Eloha, Elohim, El-Elohe-Israel,*—Genesis 33:30, and Yahweh, the latter the victorious covenant name. He is God, the LORD, Isaiah 42:8, the LORD God, splendorously endowed with trinitarian majesty. He ruled the created order, constantly baffling the Serpent's conceited religiosities. In that long and tempestuous history, he revealed magnifying names:

> He is *El-Elyon*, God Most High, Genesis 14:22; Psalms 78:35, 91:1;
> he is *Adonai*, LORD, Genesis 15:1-12; Daniel 9:3-19; Malachi 1:6;
> he is El-roi, the God of seeing, "a God who sees," Genesis 16:13;
> he is "God hears," Genesis 16:11;
> he is *El Shaddai*, God Almighty, Genesis 17:1, 28:3, 35:11; Psalm 91:1;
> he is El-olam, the Everlasting, Genesis 21:33; Malachi 3:5-7;
> he is *Jehovah Jireh*, the Provider, Genesis 22:8, 14;
> he is the God of Abraham, Genesis 24:27, 31:42, 53;
> he is God of Nahor, Genesis 31:53;
> he is the God of Bethel, Genesis 31:13;
> he is the Fear of Jacob, Genesis 31:42, 53;
> he is the God of Abraham and Isaac, Genesis 32:9;
> he is *Jehovah*, God Almighty, "I am the LORD," Exodus 6:1-3;
> he is the Healer, Exodus 15:26;
> he is David, Ezekiel 34:23-24;
> he is *Jehovah-nissi*, the LORD is My Banner, Exodus 17:8-16;

he is Jealous, Exodus 34:14; Deuteronomy 4:24, 5:9; Joshua 24:19; Nahum 1:2;
he is *Jehovah-M'Kaddish*, the Sanctifier, Leviticus 20:8;
he is God of gods and Lord of kings, Deuteronomy 10:17; Daniel 2:47;
he is the Holy One of Israel, Isaiah 41:14, 43:14;
he is *Jehovah-sabaoth*, the LORD of hosts, 1 Samuel 17:45; Haggai 2:4–9;
he is the Glory of Israel, 1 Samuel 15:29;
he is the Commander, Joshua 5:13–15;
he is Yahweh-shalom, Judges 6:24;
he is *El-berith*, the God of the covenant, Judges 9:46;
he is the Fortress, Psalm 18:2;
he is the Shepherd, Psalm 23:1;
he is the Refuge, Psalms 46:1, 91:2;
he is the Father/protector, Psalm 68:5–6;
he is the living God, Psalms 84:2;
he is the Judge, Psalm 94:2;
he is the Rock, Psalm 144:1;
he is the Creator, Isaiah 40:28;
he is the King, Psalm 5:2; Isaiah 6:5; Malachi 1:14;
he is the Immanuel,[15] Isaiah 7:14;
he is the Majestic One, Isaiah 10:34;
he is the Shoot from the stem of Jesse, Isaiah 11:1,
he is "The Lord is our righteousness," Jeremiah 23:6;
he is the Wonderful Counselor, the Mighty God, the Everlasting Father,[16]
and the Prince of Peace, Isaiah 9:6;
he is the Servant,[17] Isaiah 42:1, 52:13;[18]
he is the Redeemer, Isaiah 43:14, 47:4;
he is the First and the Last, Isaiah 43:10, 44:6, 45:5;
he is the Husband, Isaiah 54:5;[19] Hosea 2:16;

---

15. Torrance, "Being of One Substance with the Father," 49–61, in Seitz. *Nicene Christianity*, 54, "The Christian faith lives and breathes from the recognition, through the Spirit, that Jesus is Immanuel, the one in whom we meet the fullness of the Godhead dwelling bodily, giving himself to us to be known and understood and loved, the redemptive presence of the one through whom and for whom all things were created."

16. Deuteronomy 32:6b; Isaiah 63:16, 64:8; Jeremiah 3:19, 31:19, 22; Malachi 2:10; etc. A father procreates and protects; this second meaning of fatherhood defines Jesus through the Father-name.

17. God the Son's servanthood applies to his (coming) humanity, Acts 3:13, 26; etc.

18. At times, Isaiah called Israel the LORD's servant, 44:1.

19. The Maker is a plural noun with a singular verb; he immediately identified with the singular LORD of hosts, fully cognizant of the law that a wife may have only one husband.

> he is the Hope of Israel, Jeremiah 17:13;
> he is *Yahweh-tsidkenu*, the LORD is our righteousness, Jeremiah 23:6;
> he is the Branch, Jeremiah 23:5–6; Isaiah 11:1; Zechariah 3:8, 6:12;
> he is *Jehovah-shammai*, "the Lord is there," Ezekiel 48:35;
> he is the God of heaven, Daniel 2:18–19;
> he is the King of heaven, Daniel 4:37;
> he is Israel, Isaiah 49:3;
> he is the Prince of princes, Daniel 8:25;
> he is the "I Am," Isaiah 46:9;
> etc.

These names and titles, traditionally associated with God the Father, have primary reference to God the Son. 1) Throughout Scriptures, God the Son rules over that which God the Father originally planned and God the Spirit animated, Psalm 95:6–7. And 2) throughout Scriptures, God the Son reveals that he protects according to the protective care over the Church analogous familial fatherhood. Hence, Not God the Father but God the Son with the blessings of God the Father and God the Spirit comes into the foreground throughout biblical revelation.

The LORD God's name, the Name, reveals his nature and character—in Deuteronomy 28:58, terror for resisting him; in Psalm 5:11, safety; in Psalms 23:3, 119:132, shepherding care; in Psalm 61:5, divine listening; in Psalm 69:36, mercy; in Isaiah 56:6; Jeremiah 48:17, protection; in Micah 7:7, hope; etc. To be specific, the Name moves synonymously with the wide sweep of meanings that each context recommends and magnifies all ranges of the Christ's divine splendor.[20]

3

In timely situations, God the Son by means of angelic messengers testified to his authority over heaven and earth for the benefit of Israel. Often, throughout the first dispensation, he sent these messengers to direct his people to make the history of the Kingdom/Recreation, giving credence thereby to trinitarian glory in preparation for the Incarnation. So, as Eve's Seed, God the Son by ambassadorial emissaries declared his awe-inspiring omnipotence, omniscience, and omnipresence in ways radically different

---

20. At the completion of the Tabernacle, Exodus 40:34–38; Leviticus 9:23, the Temple, 1 Kings 8:10; 2 Chronicles 5:13, 7:1–3; and at the vision of the New Testament temple, Ezekiel 44:4, the overwhelming glory of the LORD overpowered specifically the Aaronic priests.

from idols, figments of reprobate imaginations, to accomplish the Genesis 3:14-19 prophecy.

The Christ-appointed angelic messengers spoke in his name and acted on his behalf to select citizens of the Kingdom/Recreation, even to people outside the covenant community. Such revelations of ambassadorial angels merit mention, either negative in judgment or positive in mercy.

> The angel of the LORD manifested mercy to Hagar because of her son fathered by Abram/Abraham, Genesis 16:7-14, 21:15-21. Ishmael received a limited blessing, Genesis 21:13, much as Esau later, Genesis 27:39-40.

> Two angels who had accompanied the Christ rescued Lot and family from under Sodom and Gomorrah's sulfurous rains of fire, Genesis 18:2, 22, 19:25-29.

> On Mount Moriah, the angel of the LORD called out to Abraham, "Do not lay your hand on the boy or do anything to him, for now I know that you fear God, seeing you have not withheld your son, your only son, from me," Genesis 22:12. Immediately upon completing the test, the LORD through this messenger repeated the full covenant blessing, Genesis 22:16-18. James 2:21-23; Hebrews 11:17-19.

> The angel of the LORD alerted Jacob to the fraud Laban and sons conspired in order to gain his wealth; at the same time, this messenger revealed the way to hold these family members at bay, Genesis 31:11.

> Jacob/Israel recognized that the angel of the LORD had over the course of his life redeemed him from all evil, indicating hereby the divine presence providentially preserving his life, Genesis 48:15-16.

> An angel of the LORD positioned himself between the closing-in Pharaonic army and the moving-out Israelite nation, Exodus 14:19.

> The LORD God appointed a divine messenger to lead Israel away from the Sinai through the wilderness, Exodus 23:20-21, 33:2. This angel with all required authority then spoke and acted totally encumbered by the burden of leadership, Exodus 23:22-28; Isaiah 63:9.

For the entire desert journey, the LORD led Israel in an angelic pillar of cloud by day and fire by night, Deuteronomy 31:15–21; Psalm 99:6–7.

The angel of the LORD first blocked Balaam's way, then opened this bribable *prophet's* eyes and addressed him judgmentally, Numbers 22:22–35. Though the angel had the greedy man's life in his hands, nevertheless he spared him for the purpose of blessing Israel. Balaam, of unenvious reputation, 2 Peter 2:15–16; Jude 11; Revelation 2:14, earned the death penalty, Numbers 31:8.

An angel of the LORD condemned Israel's unfaithfulness, Judges 2:1–4; speaking for his sender, the Christ, this messenger spread condemnation over the covenant people. And Israel as a people wept tears of repentance.

With Israel on the downgrade of unfaithfulness, the angel of the LORD manifested himself to Gideon and commanded the man to reform the Faith of the covenant nation, Judges 6:11–24.[21]

The angel of the LORD, in one of Israel's nadirs in faithlessness, prepared Manoah and his wife for Samson's birth as well as Nazirite status, Judges 13:1–25.[22]

The angel of the LORD appeared to David, confronting his prideful sinning, the myopically conceived general census. In the 2 Samuel 24 narrative, the LORD incited the king to count Israel, and in the 1 Chronicles 21 account, the Satan provoked him. The LORD God halted this messenger from fatally marring Jerusalem and placed the guilt of sinning on David, 1 Chronicles 21:17; 2 Samuel 24:17.

---

21. The angel of the LORD appeared to Gideon and addressed the man in the name of the LORD God with all ambassadorial authority. "The LORD is with you, O mighty man of valor." Again, "And the LORD turned to him and said, 'Go in this might of yours and save Israel from the hand of Midian; do not I send you?'" And again, "And the LORD said to him, 'But I will be with you, and you shall strike the Midianites as one man.'" When the angel of the LORD has completed his messaging he turned Gideon's food into a sacrifice. In between the beginning and the ending of the narrative, the angel of the LORD spoke with the representative authority of the LORD God.

22. The angel of the LORD appeared to Manoah's wife and promised her and her husband a child. Manoah spoke of the angel as a man of God, Judges 13:8–20, who identified himself as the "I am." Finished with his messaging, the angel of the Lord went up in the flame of the burnt offering that Manoah and his wife presented. Throughout the account, with a name too wonderful, this "I am" acted with total ambassadorial authority.

The angel of the LORD provided Elijah twice with victuals for the forty-day journey to the Horeb, 1 Kings 19:4–8, there to behold the glory of God the Son.

The angel of the LORD sent Elijah to stop King Ahaziah's messengers, 2 Kings 1:3–4 and made them return, carrying a painful message.

An angel of the LORD, agent of justice, mercilessly struck down 185,000 Assyrian troops, 2 Kings 19:35; 2 Chronicles 32:21; Isaiah 37:36.

Nebuchadnezzar, perplexed, saw a fourth *personage* in the fiery furnace, an angel of the LORD protecting Daniel's three friends from immolation, Daniel 3:24–30. Also, an angelic voice from heaven condemned the mighty king deluged by delusions of grandeur to seven years of animal existence, Daniel 4:31–33.

The angel of the LORD clarified for Zechariah the meaning of the men riding colored horses, Zechariah 1:9–10, which made the prophet plead for mercy, Zechariah 1:11–17.

The angel of the LORD rebuked Satan for accusing Joshua the High Priest for Israel's sins and then clothed the man in garments of righteousness, Zechariah 3:1–5. This same emissary promised the coming of the messianic Branch, Zechariah 3:6–10.

The man clothed in linen, who swore by him who lives forever, served the LORD God as messenger, Daniel 8:15–17, 10:5, 12:7. This man in linen, an angel, also appeared to Ezekiel, 9:3, 10:2.

Briefly now, angels as Gabriel, Daniel 9:20–23; Luke 1:26–38, and Michael, Daniel 12:1–3 personified the ambassadorial authority of the LORD God. This royal representation he incorporated in Psalms, 34:7, 35:5–6, 91:11; etc., that Israel, worshiping, glorify him.

4

During the first dispensation, the Preincarnate entered into the history of his people, the history of the Kingdom/Recreation with kinetic Christophanies; on each occasion, he magnified his divinity.

Adam and Eve, suddenly aware of the enormity of a single, simple sin, heard in the evening of Day Seven, the LORD God walking in the Garden, questioning the man, Genesis 3:9, "Where are you?" Though hidden, God the Son, omniscient, located the errant pair.

In the cutting of the covenant—the covenant originally revealed to Adam and to Noah—the LORD symbolized himself by a smoking fire pot and a flaming torch passing between the carcass halves; while Abram/Abraham slept, the LORD God alone with emphasis on Canaan reformed the promises and the obligations, Genesis 15:17–21.[23]

In the company of angelic escorts, also incarnate, the LORD in typically Semitic manhood pledged to Abraham and Sarah the long-promised heir, Genesis 18:1–15. The Preincarnate at one of Abraham's low points of trust in the promise of an heir gave credibility to his covenant commitment.

At the same time, when possession of Canaan seemed incredible, the LORD God as friend confided to Abraham his plans to eradicate Sodom and Gomorrah. By purging the land of all wretched evil, first these two population centers, the LORD promised the whole of Canaan to Abram/Abraham. Genesis 18:17–21,

> The LORD said, "Shall I hide from Abraham what I am about to do, seeing that Abraham shall surely become a great and mighty nation, and all the nations of the earth shall be blessed in him? For I have chosen him, that he may command his children and his household after him to keep the way of the LORD by doing righteousness and justice, so that the LORD may bring to Abraham what he has promised him?" Then the LORD said, "Because the outcry against Sodom and Gomorrah is great and their sin is very grave, I will go down to see whether they have done altogether according to the outcry that has come to me. And if not, I will know."

As a grieving friend confiding in a deep-listening companion,[24] God the Son, face to face with Abraham, unburdened himself.

With the promise of a son and by the elimination of wicked habitations, the Preincarnate visualized for doubtful Abraham his covenant future in Canaan.

The LORD issued a promise to Jacob fleeing Esau and nearing Haran. Genesis 28:12–13, "And [Jacob] dreamed, and behold, there was a ladder set up on the earth, and the top of it reached to heaven. And behold, the angels of God were ascending and descending on it! And behold, the LORD stood above it and said, 'I am the LORD, the God of Abraham your father and the God of Isaac. The land on which you lie I will give to you and to your

---

23. Jeremiah 34:18 records a similar covenant cutting ceremony.
24. Abraham as friend: Isaiah 41:8; James 2:23.

offspring.'" Thus, God the Son addressed the next-after-Abraham-and-Isaac covenant head. John 1:51.

The LORD God tested Jacob in a physical winner-take-all wrestling match; thereby he empowered the man to encounter his twice-betrayed brother, Genesis 32:22–32. At this stage in Abraham's grandson's life confidence in the twenty-year old Genesis 28:12–13 promise waned low. And at Esau's approach, the historical worth of that promise had dwindled into nihility. Then, at this unprecedented *make-or-break* center of gravity for covenant survival, the LORD revealed himself, testifying thereby the continuous reality of the earlier promise, to motivate Jacob to meet Esau. Jacob, whom the LORD God had renamed Israel, exclaimed, Genesis 32:30, "For I have seen God face to face, and yet my life has been delivered." The test result gave Jacob/Israel the trust to believe the Preincarnate.

The LORD confronted Moses journeying with his family to Egypt and nearly slew him. For Moses had ignored the circumcision mandate for his second son, which rite resenting Zipporah executed, Exodus 4:24–26.

At preparing Israel for the Exodus, the LORD ordered Moses and all the men to smear the blood of Passover lambs on the doorframes of the houses in which they ate the sacrificial sheep. Exodus 12:12–13, "For I will pass through the land of Egypt that night and I will strike all the firstborn in the land of Egypt, both man and beast; and on all the gods of Egypt I will execute judgments: I am the LORD. The blood shall be a sign for you, on the houses where you are. And when I see the blood, I will pass over you, and no plague shall befall you to destroy you, when I strike the land of Egypt." Exodus 12:29.

The glory of the LORD appeared to Israel, promising the providential manna, Exodus 16:10.

At the LORD's command, Moses, Aaron, Nadab, Abihu, and seventy Israelite elders ascended the Sinai. Exodus 24:10–11, ". . . and they saw the God of Israel. There was under his feet as it were a pavement of sapphire stone, like the very heaven for clearness. And he did not lay his hand on the chief men of the people of Israel; they beheld God, and ate and drank." As the preincarnate LORD God revealed himself, these men then testified to Israel the actuality of his glorious existence, a revelation necessary to this recently enslaved people struggling to grasp the stamina of covenant freedom.

Upon this friendship meal, the LORD ordered Moses and Joshua higher, into his glory. Exodus 24:16–18, "The glory of the LORD dwelt on Mount Sinai, and the cloud covered it six days. And on the seventh day he called to Moses out of the midst of the cloud. Now the appearance of the glory of the LORD was like a devouring fire on the top of the mountain in the sight of the people of Israel. Moses entered the cloud and went up on the mountain.

And Moses was on the mountain forty days and forty nights." Throughout these forty days and night, while Joshua waited, the LORD God gave Moses the hand-engraved Decalogue[25] and the Tabernacle's blueprint.[26]

To bring closure to the idolatrous Golden-Calf fiasco, as the Israelites rightfully feared for their existence, mediating Moses, unbidden, at the risk of his life, ascended the Sinai summit to seek atonement for a people on the edge of condemnation. As Moses questioned his leadership commission, the LORD issued a promise reconfirming the man in his office. Exodus 33:18–23,

> Moses said, "Please, show me your glory." And he said, "I will make all my goodness pass before you and will proclaim before you my name[27] 'The LORD.' And I will be gracious to whom I will be gracious, and I will show mercy on whom I will show mercy. But," he said, "You cannot see my face, for man shall not see me and live." And the LORD said, "Behold, there is a place by me where you shall stand on the rock, and while my glory passes by I will put you in a cleft of the rock, and I will cover you with my hand until I have passed by. Then I will take away my hand, and you shall see my back, but my face shall not be seen."

In this epiphany,[28] the LORD re-convicted Moses of his leadership in Israel and Israel's eventual entry into Canaan.

Once more Moses ascended Mount Sinai, this time to receive the Decalogue's duplicate. At descending, the glory of the LORD still enveloped him. Exodus 34:29, "When Moses came down from Mount Sinai, with the two tables of the testimony in his hand as he came down from the mountain, Moses did not know that the skin of his face shone because he had been talking with God." This evidence of divine goodwill convinced both Moses and Israel that the LORD God intended to lead them farther, into Canaan. Jude 5.

Israel in fear of destruction and Moses in doubt of his office now recognized 1) that the LORD God, unlike entrancing Egyptian and Canaanite gods, actually existed and 2) Moses remained the approved leader.

---

25. Exodus 31:18, 34:1–5; Deuteronomy 9:10.

26. Exodus 25:9, "Exactly as I show you concerning the pattern of the tabernacle, and all of its furniture, so you shall make it."

27. As noted earlier, the Name represents the totality of the Preincarnate's divinity.

28. According to Exodus 24:16–18, conscious Moses lived forty days and forty nights in the glorious presence of the LORD, thoroughly blessed. But according to Genesis 33:18–23, he barely survived a passing glimpse of divine majesty. In the former narration, Moses dwelt in divine mercy. In the latter account, terrifying, Israel's leader perceived the majesty of divine justice.

In sum, to prosper Moses' significance, the LORD spoke to him from the mercy seat of the ark of the covenant, Exodus 25:22, even mouth to mouth, Numbers 12:5-8.

The LORD in commissioning Joshua spoke directly to him, Deuteronomy 31:7-8, 14-15, in a manner all Israel recognized as definitive.

According to Joshua 5:13-15, God the Son, the Commander of the army of the Lord, confronted Israel's leader and prepared him for the invasion of Canaan, beginning at the Jericho road block.

First Samuel 3:1-14 narrated the Christ addressing the young man. "And the LORD came and stood, calling as at other times, 'Samuel! Samuel!'" This calling initiated a new beginning in unfaithful Israel.

Micaiah perceived the LORD, 2 Chronicles 18:16-23, 1 Kings 22:19; and declared to King Ahab, "... hear the word of the LORD: I saw the LORD sitting on his throne, and all the host of heaven standing beside him on his right hand and on his left." In this Christophany, the LORD sowed the seeds of Ahab's demise.

Elijah, in crisis mode, 1 Kings 19:10, fleeing murderous Jezebel and seeking the LORD's will, headed for isolated Horeb. To restore the prophet's faith and prophetic mandate, the LORD God addressed him. First Kings 19:11-13,

> "Go out and stand on the mount before the LORD." And behold, the LORD passed by, and a great and strong wind tore the mountains and broke in pieces the rocks before the LORD, but the LORD was not in the wind. And after the wind an earthquake, but the LORD was not in the earthquake. And after the earthquake a fire, but the LORD was not in the fire. And after the fire the sound of a low whisper. And when Elijah heard it, he wrapped his face in his cloak and went out and stood at the entrance of the cave. And behold, there came a voice to him and said, "What are you doing here, Elijah?" He said, "I have been jealous for the LORD, the God of hosts. For the people of Israel have forsaken your covenant, thrown down your altars, and killed your prophets with the sword, and I, even I only, am left, and they seek my life, to take it away." And the LORD said to him, "Go, return..."

Restored in the Faith and reanimated for prophetic ministry, the man returned to his public posting in Northern Israel, Jezebel less a feared threat.

Job, in the pit of suffering and by fighting off "friendly" accusations, confessed great *go'el* hope. Job 19:25-26,

TRINITARIAN CONFRONTATION

> For I know that my Redeemer lives,
> and that at the last he will stand upon the earth.
> And after my skin has been thus destroyed,
> yet in my flesh I shall see God.

In this abhorrent fusion of physical agonies and embittering indictments, the LORD stimulated the man with prophetic foresight.[29]

In the year King Uzziah/Azariah died, wanton Judah had again fallen into paganizing depths of idolatry, 2 Kings 15:1-7/2 Chronicles 26:1-23. In that pool of fragmenting authoritarianism, the LORD summoned Isaiah to the prophetic office and revealed himself. Exclaimed the newly commissioned prophet, Isaiah 6:1,

> ... I saw the LORD sitting upon a throne, high and lifted up; and the train of his robe filled the temple.

The Preincarnate seated upon the throne of all authority (at the right hand of the eternally invisible God the Father) moved the man into life-long action. John 12:41.

To enkindle ministry among the exiles in Babylon, the LORD God revealed himself to Ezekiel in a most uncommon vision, 1:26-28.

> And above the expanse over [the angels'] heads there was the likeness of a throne, in appearance like sapphire; and seated above the likeness of a throne was a likeness with a human appearance. And upward from what had the appearance of his waist I saw as it were gleaming metal, like the appearance of fire enclosed all around. And downward from what had the appearance of his waist I saw as it were the appearance of fire, and there was brightness around him. Like the appearance of the bow that is in the cloud on the day of rain, so was the appearance of the brightness all around. Such was the appearance of the likeness of the glory of the LORD. And when I saw it, I fell on my face, and I heard the voice of one speaking.

Now, poised for prophecy, Ezekiel recognized that by coming from the north, from Jerusalem, to the south, Babylon, the LORD God demonstrated 1) that he remembered the exiles and 2) that he, omnipresent, ruled heaven and earth. More often Ezekiel saw the LORD, as in a mirror dimly, 3:23, 9:3, 10:1-2, 8:1-4,

> In the sixth year, in the sixth month, on the fifth day of the month, as I sat in my house, with the elders of Judah sitting

---

29. Wisdom literature, as Job, is not given to historical events; Proverbs 30:4 is best interpreted as a father-son teaching relationship.

before me, the hand of the LORD God fell upon me there. Then I looked, and behold, a form that had the appearance of a man. Below what appeared to be his waist was fire, and above his waist was something like the appearance of brightness, like gleaming metal. He put out the form of a hand and took me by a lock of my head, and the Spirit lifted me up between earth and heaven and brought me in visions of God to Jerusalem, to the entrance of the gateway of the inner court that faces north, where was the seat of the image of jealousy, which provokes to jealousy. And behold, the glory of the God of Israel was there, like the vision that I saw in the valley.

With that *image* in his head, the qualified prophet proceeded anticipatorily into his ministry among a hard-hearted people.

Daniel himself perceived the Son of Man,[30] the LORD God, in a vision, 7:13–14, therewith to inspire Israel's exilic community with hope for the coming of the Kingdom/Recreation.

> I saw in the night visions,
> and behold,
> with the clouds of heaven there came one like a son of man,
> and he came to the Ancient of Days and was presented before him.
> And to him was given dominion and glory and a kingdom,
> that all peoples, nations, and languages should serve him;
> his dominion is an everlasting dominion,
> which shall not pass away,
> and his kingdom one that shall not be destroyed.

This vision of the Son of Man steadied Daniel in the midst of most horrific historical developments; he saw the presiding Judge of empires, nations, and peoples.

In sum, because of these visions and appearances, the people feared for their lives. Exodus 20:18–19, "Now when all the people saw the thunder and the flashes of lightning and the sound of the trumpet and the mountain smoking, the people were afraid and trembled, and they stood far off and said to Moses, 'You speak to us, and we will listen; but do not let God speak to us, lest we die.'" Aware of shameful guiltiness, they feared damnation. Yet, the LORD God through these revelations demonstrated mercy upon mercy.

---

30. John 5:27; etc. God the Father designated Jesus, now with his humanity and divinity, the eternal Judge. As the LORD God he had this office prior to the Incarnation; upon the Ascension, he, now human and divine, resumed his place on the great throne, judging the peoples.

5

Now, throughout the first dispensation, from Genesis 3:14–19 through Isaiah 11:1–9 to Isaiah 65:17–18, the LORD projected the eschatological stress in first-dispensation history, the whole straining with pangs of parturition to bring about the Incarnation.

> For behold,
> I create new heavens and a new earth,
> and the former things shall not be remembered or come to mind.
> But be glad and rejoice forever in that which I create;
> for behold,
> I create Jerusalem to be a joy.

At the conclusion to the first dispensation and in the doorway to the second, the Preincarnate out of the trinitarian communion voiced with divine determination the eschatological revelation of the Kingdom/Recreation. With this eschatological drive, the constituent Old Testament hope, God the Son prepared Israel for the New Testament dispensation, the fuller disclosure of the Trinity's unfathomable complexity focused on the Incarnation.

To sum up the Son's preincarnate appearances: everywhere in the Old Testament history, he revealed himself the Lord and the Savior. From the initial recreative act, Genesis 3:14–19, through the rescue of Noah's Eight, the calling of Abram/Abraham, the Exodus, Aaron's sacrifices, the Davidic monarchy, and the return from the Exile, he saved his remnant people. Isaiah 12:2; 43:11,

> I, I am the LORD,
> and besides me there is no savior.

The Working Spirit

God the Spirit breathed life into all creation; though invisible as the wind, with holy decisiveness he revealed his majestic workings, Genesis 1:2.

True to his imperceptible divinity, the Spirit gave intractable evidence of his presence. Profoundly and irresistibly active, he moved the prophets to speak, infused the dead with life, empowered the members of the Religion for service, integrated historical events for the Incarnation, and enriched the Christ in perseverance relative to the Atonement. This is to say: the authoritative Holy Spirit, communicating out from his trinitarian communion, amply confirmed his omnipotent, omniscient, and omnipresent energies.

1

Relative to prophetic ministry, the Spirit equipped many men to reveal the LORD God's dominion at constructing the Kingdom/Recreation, stirring dead bodies into life, calling the elect to confess the Faith, building the hope for the Incarnation, and inspiriting the Preincarnate to assume the taxing burden of his humanity.

Mindful of the Spirit's concentrated powers: he boosted hesitant Abraham's strengths of prophecy, Genesis 20:7, vivified Moses to announce the coming of the greater prophet, Deuteronomy 18:15–18, entered into Saul for glossolalia, 1 Samuel 10:9–13, emboldened a man of God to speak against Jeroboam, 1 Kings 13:1, sharpened another unnamed man to convict Ahab of gross error, 1 Kings 20:35–43, validated David to embrace the prophetic office, 2 Samuel 23:2/Acts 2:30, mandated Elijah to charge Northern Israel with idolatry, 1 Kings 17:1–2, and compelled Elisha to take up Elijah's mantel, 1 Kings 19:19—2 Kings 13:21, all the while visible only in his workings.

Similarly, without exposing his divinity, the Spirit of God called others to the prophetic office: Micaiah, 1 Kings 22:1–28/2 Chronicles 18:7, 12; Amasai, 1 Chronicles 12:18; Azariah, 2 Chronicles 15:1–8; Nathan, 2 Samuel 12:1–15; 1 Kings 1:22–23, 1:38, 1 Chronicles 17:1, 29:29; Gad, 2 Samuel 24:18–19, 1 Chronicles 29:29; Oded, 2 Chronicles 28:9; Uriah, Jeremiah 26:20; etc. These Spirit-endowed men, with Isaiah, Jeremiah, Ezekiel, Daniel, Hosea, Joel, Amos, Obadiah, Jonah, Micah, Nahum, Habakkuk, Zephaniah, Haggai (Ezra 5:1), Zechariah (Ezra 5:1), and Malachi, in minor and major ways spoke prophetically to lead the Old Testament Church towards the focal point of the first dispensation.[31]

Throughout the Old Testament dispensation, the Spirit juxtaposed Christ-commissioned men, and several informed women,[32]—to the in Deuteronomy 13:1–5 exposed false prophets. Spirit-gifted prophets actually foretold in the forthtelling of Israelite history the way, the truth, and the life of the Incarnation. Through these men, even as the seventy appointed according to Numbers 11:16–25, 26–30, the Spirit commanded the Old Church to acknowledge what the Apostle later declared, 2 Peter 1:21, "For no prophecy was ever produced by the will of man, but men spoke from God as they were carried along by the Holy Spirit." Pointedly, God the Spirit animated duly commissioned men to call the future into the present, opening the tomorrow doors, 2 Peter 3:11–12.

---

31. The court prophets in 1 Kings 22, the one in 1 Kings 13:18–19, and those of Jeremiah 23:25 sought to impede the way and work of the LORD.

32. Miriam, Exodus 15:20; Deborah, Judges 4:4; and Huldah, 2 Kings 22:14.

2

Always, the Spirit in his life-expansive ministry worked in tandem with God the Father and God the Son; for this reason, he vested many with resolute authority to serve, magnifying him:

> He qualified Bezalel, son of Uri, with uncommon skills for Tabernacle construction, Exodus 31:3, 35:31.
>
> He separated Israelites of well-grounded stature to assist in Moses' teaching ministry, Numbers 11:16–30.
>
> He *swayed* Balaam, bribable man, to prophesy great blessings upon Israel, Numbers 24:2.
>
> He stirred Joshua, son of Nun, to lead Israel through the flooded Jordan into Canaan, Numbers 27:18.
>
> He promised another Spirit-oriented prophet even more capable than Moses, Deuteronomy 18:15/Acts 3:22, 7:37.
>
> He blessed men during the Judges-era to raise Israelite tribes in praise to the LORD—Othniel, Judges 3:10; Gideon, Judges 6:34; Jephthah, Judges 11:29, and of all people, Samson, Judges 13:25, 14:19, 15:14.
>
> He vivified Saul who in a company of prophets praised the LORD, 1 Samuel 10:6–10, 19:18–24.
>
> He entrusted David with leadership authority, 1 Samuel 16:13; 2 Samuel 23:2; Psalm 143:10.
>
> He answered repentant David's plea for reformation of life with mounting hope, Psalm 51:11.
>
> He gave Amasai praise-speech with which to laud David's monarchy, 1 Chronicles 12:18.
>
> He allocated prophetic insight to Azariah, 2 Chronicles 15:1–2, Jahaziel, 2 Chronicles 20:14, and Zechariah, 2 Chronicles 24:20.
>
> He recounted his historical presence in Israel exiting Egypt, Nehemiah 9:20.
>
> He divulged wisdom to Elihu, another of Job's friends, this one more substantial in truth-speaking, Job 33:4.

> He prophesied new life for Israel, for the land of Canaan too, Isaiah 32:15, 44:3.[33]
>
> He replaced in Israel hearts of stone with hearts of flesh, Ezekiel 36:27.

These interacting historical interfaces anchored the Spirit's intratrinitarian boundlessness deep into the Old Testament ages and peoples, imputing believers individually and communally with animated service.[34]

Furthermore, for this service, the Spirit pressed Israel's vision into successive tomorrows, of which several openings into the New Testament Scriptures: Psalm 2:1–2[35]/Acts 4:25–26; Psalms 69:25, 109:8/Acts 1:20; Joel 2:28–29/Acts 2:16–21; Psalm 16:8–11/Acts 2:25–28; Psalm 110:1[36]/Acts

---

33. This life-giving authority of the Holy Spirit entered also into the natural world,
> When you send forth your Spirit,
> [creatures] are created,
> and you renew the face of the ground.
> Psalm 104:30

34. At another stage in Isaiah's ministry, the preincarnate God the Son prophesied in Israel, promising the Holy Spirit for the New Testament revelation:
> For I will pour water on the thirsty land,
> and streams on the dry ground;
> I will pour my Spirit upon your offspring,
> and my blessing on your descendants.
> Isaiah 44:3

35. Through Psalm 2, David magnified the Preincarnate who had enthroned him with an authority difficult to underestimate. From the Jerusalem throne, he summoned the monarchs of the earth to acknowledge his divinely imposed rule. The Psalm at the same time consisted of a prophecy by which God the Son points to his post-Ascension millennial reign.

At the beginning of Jesus' millennial rule, God the Father had transposed the Psalm to signify the Incarnate ruling at his right hand, Acts 4:25–26, 13:33. Hence, references as 1 Corinthians 15:25, Hebrews 1:13, 10:13, and Revelation 12:1–6 glorify Christ Jesus.

Hence, Evangelical translators/interpreters of Psalm 2, by explicating it as a direct prophecy centered on the LORD God, eisegete.

36. The preposition in Psalm 110's *A Psalm of David* carries a wide range of interpretive meanings, each controlled by its context. Since an anonymous third party authored this psalm, the prepositional sense connotes *concerning, for*—hence *A Psalm concerning* or *for David*. Now the first line reads, *The LORD says to [David]*. In effect, the Preincarnate spoke to Israel's king.

In the New Testament, the omnipotent Incarnate addressed David whom he had enthroned, Matthew 22:43; Mark 12:36; Luke 20:42, and the Apostles followed him in recognizing the renowned king's authority, Acts 2:34. This is to say, Jesus as well as his apostles recognized the criticality of David's monarchy.

In deference of the anonymous composer, others than David contributed to the psalm collection—Solomon, #72; Asaph, #73–83; sons of Korah, #84, 85, 87, 88; Ethan the Ezrahite, #89; Moses, #90. The unknown composer thus fits in; he praised David in

2:34; in more and masterful ways the Holy Spirit empowered multiple elect to interpret the past in the present for the coming ages.

3

Conversely, the Spirit's absence terminated the will to serve as well as the capacity to believe the Trinity. For this various illustrations. Genesis 6:3 recorded God the Son's regret at creating the Adamites, Adam's now unbelieving, Spirit-less, descendants. Therefore the LORD cleansed the earth with the massively destructive violence of the Flood. Similarly, when the Spirit withdrew from King Saul, the man died, 1 Samuel 16:14. Zedekiah, son of Chenaanah, in the name of the Spirit blasphemed, and expired, 1 Kings 22:24. Nehemiah, 9:30, declared that the Spirit by way of the prophets had addressed Israel in vain, leaving the many wretched in revolutionary debris. Isaiah 6:9–10/Acts 28:26–27 flagged the cause of the Jews' condemnation.

For grieving the Spirit became Israel's unforgiveable sin, Isaiah 63:10, a condemnation that Zechariah repeated, 7:12a, "They made their hearts diamond-hard lest they should hear the laws and the words that the LORD of hosts has sent by his Spirit through the former prophets." Revolting against the Spirit brought about inflammatory evidence for Old Israel's descent into unfaithfulness and doom—to create room for the New Israel.

At the Spirit's withdrawal from the covenant community, the people invariably believed falsehood and, hardened in sin, died.

4

Notably, Isaiah in decisive instances foretold the Holy Spirit's creative presence in preincarnate God the Son.

> And the Spirit of the LORD shall rest upon him,
> the Spirit of wisdom and understanding,
> the Spirit of counsel and might,
> the Spirit of knowledge and the fear of the LORD.
> Isaiah 11:2/Matthew 3:16; Mark 1:10; Luke 3:22
>
> Behold my servant,
> whom I (God the Father) uphold,
> my chosen,

---

his service to the LORD and for the potency of his royal authority.

Evangelical translators/interpreters of Psalm 110, by explicating it as a direct prophecy centered on the LORD God, eisegete.

> in whom is my soul delights;
> I have put my Spirit upon him;
> he will bring forth justice to the nations.
> He will not cry aloud or lift up his voice,
> or make it heard in the street;
> a bruised reed he will not break,
> and a faintly burning wick he will not quench;
> he will faithfully bring forth justice.
> He will not grow faint or be discouraged
> till he has established justice in the earth;
> and the coastlands wait for his law.
> Isaiah 42:1–4/Matthew 12:18–21

> The Spirit of the LORD God is upon me,
> because the LORD has anointed me
> to bring good news to the poor;
> he has sent me to bind up the broken-hearted,
> to proclaim liberty to the captives,
> and the opening of the prison to those who are bound;
> to proclaim the year of the LORD's favor,[37]
> and the day of vengeance of our God;
> to comfort all who mourn;
> to grant to those who mourn in Zion—
> to give them a beautiful headdress instead of ashes,
> the oil of gladness instead of mourning,
> the garment of praise instead of a faint spirit;
> that they may be called oaks of righteousness,
> the planting of the LORD,
> that he may be glorified.
> They shall build up the ancient ruins;
> they shall raise up the former devastations;
> they shall repair the ruined cities,
> the devastations of many generations.
> Isaiah 61:1–4/Luke 4:18–19

With these Isaian passages, God the Father addressed the Spirit-anointed Preincarnate who acknowledged the indwelling Spirit. Matthew 3:13–17; Mark 1:9–10; Luke 3:21–22.

---

37. Here Jesus stopped quoting from this Isaian passage, Luke 4:19.

Second Summation

From Day One, the Three-of-the-Trinity *worked* tirelessly, first creating the universe. Then, upon the Adamic Fall, they initiated the reformation of the Kingdom/Recreation. The Trinity endowed this reformation with captivating urgency, for which God the Son entered the created order and bonded with humanity, thus defining Jesus. Thereupon, with the eschatological haste of the Crucifixion-Resurrection-Ascension, the Divinity synchronized all historical events, destination locked onto the Eschaton.

Over millennia and with Israel, the Savior God created the nucleus of the new universe; he recreated the Genesis 3:14–15 Gospel, forever proclaiming the truth of Exodus 20:2/Deuteronomy 5:6, "I am the LORD your God, who brought out of the land of Egypt, out of the house of slavery." To materialize this evolving Gospel, he issued the Decalogue, the way of perennial peace. On that way, he provided the essential goods—food, water, and space—so that Israel stood out in the international order as the hope of the nations.

Over the Old Testament dispensation and foundational for the New, the invisible Trinity through the work of the Preincarnate created the history of the world. For Israel and in Israel, the Three-in-One day-by-day powered all historical events to achieve the Incarnation. With determined willpower, the One-in-Three thus moved history to the first and great Judgment,[38] eventually also the second and last Judgment, Revelation 20:11–15, then the Parousia, the eternal magnification of the Divinity. For now, God the Father plans this glorification. God the Son executes this glorification. And God the Spirit blows the breath of life into this glorification. The Three-in-Unity from out of eternity validate the splendors of the new creation, in the Old Testament history the people of Israel the evidence.

---

38. Farrow, Douglas, "Confessing Christ Coming," 133–48, in Seitz. *Nicene Christianity*,144, "The one who will judge both the living and the dead is the one who died for those still living and who lives for those already dead. Certainly the judgment he will exercise will be entirely consistent with the judgment he *did* exercise, when out of unfathomable love he became . . . the Judge judged in our place."

Three

TRINITARIAN EXALTATION

When the LORD God closed off the Old Testament era, darkness dominated the created order; little to nothing remained of the Davidic Kingdom/Recreation glories, except for an insignificant remnant loosely gathered about Zechariah and Elizabeth, Joseph and Mary, and John the Baptizer. At revealing God the Father's groundwork, God the Son opened the second dispensation and turned higher the light of hope based on Genesis 3:14–19. The Gospel now glowed with trinitarian fluorescence; in that brighter scintillation, the Divinity—God the Father, God the Son, and God the Spirit—revealed himself more distinguishably than in the Old Testament writings. All New Testament documents bear witness to this consummating trinitarian unity and multiplicity—like a bud mysteriously unfolding into bloom—and enlightened the Church for magnifying the Trinity.

I-II

TRINITARIAN REVELATION

In the heartening newness of the second dispensation, Jesus' incarnational and baptismal narratives bear out the Divinity's workings with illuminating clarity. For God the Father, God the Son, and God the Spirit in eternity *assigned* each other specific tasks in a manner believable by rational creatures.

In the New Testament writings, then, the Three-of-the-Trinity disclosed essential equality, the one no more and no less divine than the others.[1]

Incarnational Revelation

Scriptures' Author/authors entrusted the Church with potent incarnational accounts, to express the inexpressible. Throughout, the Divinity activated the long-promised and joyous Incarnation at the moment of Mary's insemination.[2] This innovative and cooperative working God the Father had prophetically and constructively aligned throughout geopolitical history, Galatians 4:4–5, in order that the Three-in-One ignite the New Church's heart with trinitarian praises.

1

According to the Matthean account, God the Spirit dominated the incarnational moment. An angel to Joseph, Mary's betrothed, Matthew 1:20–23, "'... do not fear to take Mary as your wife, for that which is conceived in her is from the Holy Spirit. She will bear a son, and you shall call his name Jesus, for he will save his people from their sins.' All this took place to fulfill what the Lord had spoken by the prophet:

> Behold, the virgin shall conceive and bear a son,
> and they shall call his name Immanuel

(which means, God with us)." As the Spirit breathed life into Jesus' humanity—humanity of Davidic lineage—this conception settled Isaiah 7:14b immovably in the Faith, the cruciality of the Incarnation basic to Christianity. The humanly incomprehensible bonding of the invisible divinity of God the Son with the visible humanity of the Son of God made Jesus actually Jesus.

2

According to the Lucan narrative, at the critical moment of impregnation, God the Father and God the Spirit bonded God the Son to the humanity of a human being; more intensively, God the Son consciously and freely

---

1. This unity-in-divinity captures, at the very minimum, the essence of the Athanasian Creed.

2. The analogical language of insemination, impregnation, and conception in no wise even remotely penetrates incarnational secrecies.

committed himself to this embodying—divinity hence eternally bound to humanity—for creating the Incarnation. To materialize the Incarnation, Gabriel to virginal Mary, Luke 1:31–33, 35,

> ... you will conceive in your womb and bear a son,
> and you shall call his name Jesus.
> He will be great and will be called the Son of the Most High.
> And the Lord God will give to him the throne of his father
> David,
> and he will reign over the house of Jacob forever,
> and of his kingdom there will be no end.
> The Holy Spirit will come upon you,
> and the power of the Most High will overshadow you;
> therefore, the child to be born will be called holy—
> the Son of God.[3]

Mary wholeheartedly assented to this impregnation. Luke 1:38, "Behold, I am the servant of the Lord; let it be to me according to your word." In this manner, she entered into the incarnational mystery, the worst of which a sword piercing her mother heart, Luke 2:34–35.

For the impregnation, God the Father originated the insemination, God the Spirit animated this humanity, and God the Son with his divinity bonded to his humanity started on the way of humiliation, the fact-based logic of which the graced-based substitutionary atonement, Titus 2:13. Purposefully, God the Son through his impenetrable enfleshment[4] entered into the history of the created order—grace-work to which the Three-of-the-Trinity passionately and unreservedly devoted.

3

Then, in the Fourth Gospel, Apostle John summed up the historical concretion of the divine-human unity, John 1:14, "And the Word [embodied

---

3. In the Lucan incarnation account appeared the first ever name of God the Son as the Son of God, a name hitherto impossible and impermissible. The name, God the Son identifies exclusively his divinity; in distinction, the Son-of-God naming focusses on Jesus' two natures, the human and the divine—the divine leading the human into the humiliation of the Crucifixion and onto the exaltation of the Resurrection.

4. Poythress. *The Mystery of the Trinity*, 11, "He is fully human, with a full and complete human nature. He is also fully divine, with a full and complete divine nature. He is God and man. This joining of two natures in one person is a deep mystery."

himself in]⁵ flesh and dwelt among us,⁶ and we have seen his glory, glory as of the only Son from the Father, full of grace and truth." With the eternal bonding of the two wholly incompatible natures, the Trinity unambiguously created Jesus Jesus. Hence, in the spatial realm of the Incarnation, the "only-begotten"⁷ (*monogenous*) of John 1:14, 18, 3:16, disclosed the historic hope intrinsic to the vicarious atonement. And the Apostle persuasively repeated the life-giving authority of that enfleshment, 1 John 1:1–4, 4:2–3.

4

Apostle Paul voiced the seminal sense of the Incarnation directly. Romans 8:3b-4. "By sending his own Son in the likeness of sinful flesh and for sin, he condemned sin in the flesh, in order that the righteous requirement of the law might be fulfilled in us, who walk not according to the flesh but according to the Spirit." Thus, Jesus' sinless humanity suffered the consequences of sinning humanity, for which Jesus *discounted* his divinity.

By *discounting* as well as maintaining his divinity, God the Son *poured* himself into, took hold of, embedded himself in, from the moment of that conception bonded with the humanity of a male while holding on to his omnipresence, that excellence without borders.

> Have this mind among yourselves, which is yours in Christ Jesus, who, though he was in the form of God, did not count equality with God a thing to be grasped, but made himself nothing, taking the form of a servant, being born in the likeness of men. And being found in human form, he humbled himself by becoming obedient to the point of death, even death on a cross. Philippians 2:5–8

With his all-pervading divinity, Jesus moved onto the way of humiliation,⁸ strengthening his humanity for the hellish agonies of the Crucifixion. Also,

---

5. White. *The Forgotten Trinity*, 56, "Here John uses *egeneto*, a verb that refers to an action in time. And the reason is clear; the Word entered into human existence, 'became flesh,' at a particular point in time."

6. Athanasius, "Orations against the Arians," Book 1, 63–129, in Rush. *Sources of Early Christian Thought: The Trinitarian Controversy*, 74, "[Scriptures] proclaim nothing less than the everlasting and eternal nature of the Son, while they signify that he is God."

7. White. *The Forgotten Trinity*, 58, "While the traditional translation is 'only-begotten,' a better translation would be 'unique' or 'one of a kind.'"

8. White. *The Forgotten Trinity*, 89, "The Son had voluntarily . . . laid aside His divine prerogatives and *humbled* himself by entering into human flesh." 125, "This is something that Christ did himself."

pertinent with respect to the Pauline recording of the Incarnation, the force of Colossians 1:19 compels acceptance of the Incarnation. "For in him the whole fullness of deity dwells bodily." Without loss to his divinity, God the Son's omnipresence eternally filled and overflowed his humanity.

5

To voice the inexpressible riches of the Incarnation, the Author/author of the Letter to the Hebrews, 2:14–16, with situational awareness interpreted its rippling effects for later generations.

> Since therefore the children share in flesh and blood, he himself likewise partook of the same things, that through death he might destroy the one who has the power of death, that is, the devil, and deliver all those who through fear of death were subject to lifelong slavery. For surely it is not angels that he helps, but he helps the offspring of Abraham.

The Spirit's exegesis of the Incarnation maintains its sweep throughout the ages and generations. Also, he expresses the glory of the Incarnation in terms of Old Testament psalmody, Hebrews 10:5–7[9]/Psalm 40:6–8.

> Sacrifices and offerings you have not desired,
> but a body have you prepared for me;
> in burnt offerings and sin offerings you have taken no pleasure.
> Then I said,
> "Behold, I have come to do your will, O God.
> as it is written of me in the scroll of the book."[10]

From within the trinitarian communion, God the Son spontaneously committed himself to be at one with the people whom God the Father delegated to him and whom God the Spirit blessed with eternal life.

---

9. Hebrews 10:5–7 expresses its Septuagint translation.

10. The "scroll of the book" may refer to Deuteronomy 17:14–20 or to an Old Testament expression of the book of life mentioned in Luke 10:20; Philippians 4:3; etc. Psalm 139:16 lays open intricacies of such predestinarian omniscience. Whether Deuteronomy 17:14–20 or the book of life, both vivify first David's committal of heart to govern in the name of the LORD God and second Jesus' ultimacy of love.

TRINITARIAN EXALTATION

6

With the Incarnation, the foreknowing[11] Three-of-the-Trinity committed one, God the Son, to bond with a space-time bound man. First Peter 1:20–21, "He was foreknown before the foundation of the world but was made manifest in the last times for the sake of you who through him are believers in God, who raised him from the dead and gave him glory, so that your faith and hope are in God." As Mary's Son, his humanity indisputably subordinate to his divinity, he in and with that humanity paid the ransom adequate for all thereto chosen.

7

Once more, blessed beyond measure, Apostle John envisioned almighty works of grace that enlightened the Incarnation, inspiring numbness of wonder.

> And a great sign appeared in heaven, a woman clothed with the sun, with the moon under her feet, and on her head a crown of twelve stars.[12] She was pregnant and was crying out in birth pains and the agony of giving birth. And another sign appeared in heaven: behold a great red dragon with seven heads and ten horns, and on his heads seven diadems. His tail swept down a third of the stars of heaven and cast them to the earth. And the dragon stood before the woman who was about to give birth, so that when she bore her child he might devour it. She gave birth to a male child, one who is to rule all the nations with a rod of iron, but her child was caught up to God and to his throne, and the woman fled into the wilderness, where she has a place prepared by God, in which she was to be nourished for 1,260 days. Revelation 12:1–6

With awing praise, the Church reads and reflects on the celestial significance of the Incarnation.

The Incarnation occurred without divinizing Jesus' humanity or humanizing his divinity; each, his humanity and his divinity, retained its own nature, the whole inspiring greater wonderment and reverence. Summing

---

11. Rhodes. *Christ Before the Manger,* 35, "Only of Christ can it be said that his birth did not signal the beginning of his existence. Prior to his birth, he had existed for all eternity with the Father and the Holy Spirit."

12. Hendriksen. *More than Conquerors,* 164, "Now on earth this church may appear ever so insignificant and worthy of scorn and ridicule; from the aspect of *heaven* this same church is all-glorious: all that heaven can contribute of glory and of splendor is lavished upon her."

up, the inexpressibility of the Incarnation articulates exultation, which the Church confesses, simply:

> ... [he] was conceived by the Holy Spirit,
> and born of the virgin Mary.

Baptismal Revelation

In his thirtieth year and at the hour God the Father set, Jesus generated the historical moment of his intertrinitarian baptism. One day, he notified John the Baptizer to seize *the* signifying interaction of his ministry, John 1:29; the next day, in a communal place, he submitted himself to this sacramental rite. Apostle John, 1:32–33, registered that to which the Baptizer bore witness. "I saw the Spirit descend from heaven like a dove, and it remained on him. I myself did not know him, but he who sent me to baptize with water said to me, 'He on whom you see the Spirit descend and remain, this is he who baptizes with the Holy Spirit.' And I have seen and have borne witness that this is the Son of God." Herewith then the scriptural Author/author recorded this vital convergence of the Baptizer and the Savior in the Church's history.

Luke, 3:21–22, Mark, 1:9–11, and Matthew, 3:13–17, composed the description of Jesus' baptism in narrative form.

> Then Jesus came from Galilee to the Jordan to John, to be baptized by him. John would have prevented him, saying, "I need to be baptized by you, and do you come to me?" But Jesus answered him, "Let it be so now, for thus it is fitting for us to fulfill all righteousness." Then he consented. And when Jesus was baptized, immediately he went up from the water, and behold, the heavens were opened to him, and he saw the Spirit of God descending like a dove and coming to rest on him; and behold, a voice from heaven said, "This is my beloved Son, with whom I am well pleased."

The Holy Spirit like a dove, according to Luke "in bodily form," settled upon Jesus, to qualify his human nature for extremes in humiliation.

In that baptismal immersion, John submersed sinless[13] Jesus into the Pharisaism/Sadduceism of Israel; the Son of God took upon himself the astronomical burdens of guilt his people had earned, alone to make the atonement,

---

13. Second Corinthians 5:21; Hebrews 4:15; 1 Peter 1:19, 2:22; 1 John 3:5.

offering satisfaction for the culpability of every sort of self-righteous activity incurred by all God the Father entrusted to him, the Lord and the Savior.

Matthew, Mark, Luke, and John in the declarative manner composed the account of Jesus' baptism. Is not this the animation of Matthew 4:17; Mark 1:15? "The time is fulfilled, and the kingdom of God is at hand; repent and believe in the gospel." In the superlative sovereignty of the Trinity, in the overpowering holiness of his divinity, Jesus commenced walking the long road to Golgotha, repeatedly revealing the Gospel's authority.

II-II

TRINITARIAN REVELATION

Early in the second dispensation, Scriptures' Author/authors disclosed basic trinitarian workings constitutive of the Kingdom/Recreation. Amidst multitudinous religiosities, foremost imperialistic Roman polytheism and gatekeeping Pharisaic/Sadduceic monotheism, Jesus majestically reformed the foundation of the Kingdom/Recreation. Through the one trinitarian will and work with which the Divinity had created the first universe, Jesus, active in the Spirit and committed to God the Father's planning, on the Davidic bedrock rebuilt the new and more glorious creation in which to make the Church and her people come alive, exalting the Trinity.

Biblically, the Trinity opened up the New Testament for the Church's simultaneous exaltation of God the Father, God the Son, and God the Spirit.

God the Father's Exaltation

Despite the Serpent's mad contentions with and through the religiosities, the New Testament Scriptures revealed that the omnipotent God the Father stunningly designed the basics of the first creation.

1

For concretizing the first universe, God the Father *innovated* the groundplan. Eternally invisible within vibrant splendors of infinity, he *wrote out* these fundamentals, according to which divine patterning he established the essentials for the Genesis creation.

1–2

Sovereign Lord,
who [designed]¹⁴ the heaven and the earth and the sea and
everything in them, . . .
Acts 4:24

. . . there is one God, the Father,
from whom are all things and for whom we exist,
and one Lord, Jesus Christ,
through whom are all things and through whom we exist.
First Corinthians 8:6

Worthy are you, our Lord and God,
to receive glory and honor and power,
for you created all things,
and *by your will* (italics added) they existed and were created.
Revelation 4:11

As *decided* in the eternality of the trinitarian communion, the Three-in-One willed that God the Father produce the blueprint for the created order. In the Corinthian passage, the Father with authority, honor, and glory projected the creation of the first universe. And in The Revelation statement, God the Father expressed his will for the first creation. To be sure, no hierarchy debased the trinitarian unity; the Father and the Son cooperated, without excluding the animating presence of God the Spirit, to create the first universe.

New Testament Author/authors disclosed as Scriptures that all constituents of the first creation—rational, animal, and vegetal—gained life to praise the founding God the Father, lest malevolent gods and goddesses sneaking out of imaginary universes arrogate that honor and glory for fraudulent ends.

Moreover, to the point, God the Father in the omnipresence of God the Son and God the Spirit, the One-in-Three equal in all excellences, revealed the authoritative planning for the first creation, the covetousness-engulfed milieu in which to establish the Kingdom/Recreation. The creation of the first universe gave God the Father the credibility in the Church for believing this authority to found the new universe. John, 10:37–38, 14:11, manifested the Father's concretized groundplan for the Kingdom/Recreation.

2–2

---

14. *Poiw* opens to many interpretations; *designed* conforms to God the Father's work.

Next, Scriptures also reveal that God the Father laid the secure substratum for the Kingdom/Recreation.

> . . . this Jesus,
> delivered up according to the definite plan and foreknowledge
> of God,
> you crucified and killed by the hands of lawless men.
> Acts 2:23

> . . . the Gentiles and the peoples of Israel,
> to do whatever your hand and your plan had predestined to
> take place.
> Acts 4:28

> . . . in these last days [God] has spoken to us by his Son,
> whom he appointed the heir of all things,
> through whom also he created the world.
> Hebrews 1:1–2

> . . . the woman fled into the wilderness,
> where she has a place prepared by God,
> in which she is to be nourished for 1,260 days.
> Revelation 12:6

On God the Father's foundation, Jesus builds the Kingdom/Recreation into which God the Spirit invincibly breathes eternal life. The Trinity ensures that these new heavens and new earth shall persevere forever and ever.

2

Matthew, 2:15; Exodus 4:22/Hosea 11:1, recorded an event of God the Father's governing authority with respect to the Kingdom/Recreation: when the Herodian turbulences of murder faded, he called Joseph and Mary with Jesus out of an Egyptian refuge for reentering Canaan-homelands.

3

According to his human nature, Jesus knew constrictions other than physical, mental, and emotional fatigue. Of these other boundaries the best known became God the Father's control to conclude the second dispensation. Matthew 24:36; Mark 13:32, ". . . concerning that day or that hour, no one knows, not even the angels in heaven, nor the Son, but only the Father." For God the Father alone out of his divine foreknowledge prescribed the eschatological conclusion to Jesus' Kingdom/Recreation, Acts 17:31; 1

Timothy 6:14. In that hour, the Lord and Savior leads the new creation into the Trinity-exulting glories of the Eschaton.

Jesus addressed another such constraint to the Twelve, Acts 1:7, "It is not for you to know times or seasons that the Father has fixed by his own authority."

God the Father retained various decisions apart from Jesus' humanity, always fastening limitations to its servant-status.

4

Once in the second dispensation, early, God the Father *appeared*, the superbly Enthroned, reminiscent of Daniel 7:9–10. Revelation 4:2–3, "... [John] was in the Spirit, and behold, a throne stood in heaven, with one seated on the throne. And he who sat there had the appearance of jasper and carnelian, and around the throne was a rainbow that had the appearance of an emerald." Now, throughout the second dispensation, God the Father hereby reveals his divine authority in the design of this age, most notably over the foundation of the Kingdom/Recreation; thereby he visualizes for all of every congregation the immensely divine groundwork on which the Lord Jesus continually reforms the new universe, central evidence of which the Church.

5

Jesus, teaching, placed God the Father at the crux of his ministry: the Father set the standard for rewarding faithfulness—out of grace. Mark 8:38; Luke 12:8–9; Matthew 16:27, "For the Son of Man is going to come with his angels in the glory of his Father and then he will repay each person according to what he has done." Such allocation of recompense applied equally to ranking. Mark 10:40; Matthew 20:23, "... to sit at my right hand and at my left is not mine to grant, but it is for those for whom it has been prepared by my Father." God the Father in the community of the Divinity prepared from eternity rewards for all who followed and follow Jesus in the Faith. Matthew 6:1, 4b, "... your Father who sees in secret will reward you." Comparatively, Daniel 12:2/John 5:26–29, "For as the Father has life in himself, so he has granted the Son also to have life in himself. And he has given him authority to execute judgment, because he is the Son of Man. Do not marvel at this, for an hour is coming when all who are in the tombs will hear [Jesus'] voice and come out, those how have done good to the resurrection of life, and those who have done evil to the resurrection of the judgment." To example these provisions of mercy and shame, the conclusion to the Parable of the Talents illustrates most directly the incentivizing of the Church, Matthew 25:14–30; Luke 19:11–27. And the Parable of the Final Judgment motivates even more, Matthew 25:31–46. Believers thus *prove* they are in Christ, Philippians 2:12–13, "... for it is God who works in you, both to will and to work for his good pleasure." Christ Jesus now in and with his humanity judges according to God the Father's eternal reckoning.

6

Scriptures reveal that in the trinitarian communion God the Father sent God the Son and God the Son makes God the Father known, a holy interactivity God the Spirit confirms in the Faith.

1–2

Throughout his ministry years, Jesus acknowledged the hierarchy between his humanity and God the Father's divinity; in his humanity, Jesus knew subordination, forever commitment to servant-status, his sinless will totally aligned with his divinity. In this servanthood, Jesus recognized God the Father's sending, a directing less prominent in the Synoptics, Matthew 10:40; Luke 4:18, 9:48, but very conspicuous in the Fourth Gospel. Repeatedly, John accentuated that God the Father sent Jesus into the world—the world as defined by the Apostle, Israel.

> John 3:17, 5:37a, "And the Father who sent me has himself borne witness about me."
>
> John 6:57, 8:26, "I have much to say about you and much to judge, but he who sent me is true, and I declare to [Israel] what I have heard from him."
>
> John 8:28–29, "When you have lifted up the Son of Man, then you will know that I am he, and that I do nothing on my own authority, but speak just as the Father taught me. And he who sent me is with me. He has not left me alone, for I always do the things that are pleasing to him."
>
> John 3:13, 6:33, 38, 46, 51, 62, 8:23, 42, 9:4a, 12:44–45, 48, 13:3, 20, 14:24, 16:5, 28, 17:3; etc.

The emphatic Apostle, late first-century AD, rebutted a Pharisaic resurgence at ensnaring believers into the Tradition of the Elders and abject submission to the Oral Law. In this way, the Apostle hammered home among Jesus' followers the escape to the Pharisaic snare: God the Father validated the Christ in his ministry.

Jesus' servant-identification revealed the functioning of his humanity. Throughout, then, the Church recognized the subordinate service of Jesus' humanity. Luke too in the Acts, 3:26, pounded into the Faith the similar Gospel: Jesus is the Christ, the Son of God who defeated the Pharisaic god, and returned to the Father who sent him.

Scriptures also reveal Jesus' human submission to the Father through lamb-imagery, John 1:29, 36; 1 Peter 1:19; Revelation 5:6–10. As the resurrected and ascended Jesus, he took the scroll from the invisible Father's hand. Then with his eternally bonded humanity/divinity, he governed the universe, the world, the Kingdom/Recreation, and the Church according to the scroll's groundplan. The taking and the giving of the scroll forever symbolized the hierarchy between the Father's divinity and the Son's humanity, also between the Spirit's divinity and Jesus' humanity.

On account of his humanity, Jesus in all humbleness confessed that of the two the Father is the greater.

> John 14:28, "You heard me say to you, 'I am going away, and I will come to you.' If you loved me, you would have rejoiced, because I am going to the Father, for the Father is greater than I."
> John 16:28, "I came from the Father and have come into [Israel], and now I am leaving [Israel] and going to the Father."

The immense dissimilarity between the Father and Jesus' resurrected/ascended humanity formulated the hierarchy the New Church confesses.

2–2

As God the Father sent God the Son, God the Son, conversely, made God the Father known. To know God the Father means knowing his works in the elementary construction of the Kingdom/Recreation, the Incarnation, the propitiation of the Crucifixion, the Resurrection,[15] and the Ascension, even the confirmation of Jesus' rule at his right hand.

> Matthew 10:40, "Whoever receives you receives me, and whoever receives me receives him who sent me."
>
> Mark 9:37, "Whoever receives one such child in my name receives me, and whoever receives me, receives not me but him who sent me."

---

15. Poythress. *The Mystery of the Trinity*, 21, ". . . the resurrection of Christ provides an open display of the majesty of God."

Luke 10:21; Matthew 11:27, "All things have been handed over to me by my Father, and no one knows the Son except the Father, and no one knows the Father except the Son and anyone to whom the Son chooses to reveal him."

John 1:18, "No one has ever see God; the only God, who is at the Father's side, he has made him known."

John 6:38, "For I have come down from heaven, not to do my own will but the will of him who sent me."

John 6:46, ". . . not that anyone has seen the Father except he who is from God; he has seen the Father."

John 12:44, "Whoever believes in me, believes not in me but in him who sent me."

John 12:45, "And whoever sees me sees him who sent me."

John 17:6a, Jesus to God the Father, "I have manifested your name to the people whom you gave me out of [Israel]."

Etc.

In the John 14:1–14 passage, John recorded that Apostle Philip came to Jesus seeking the way to God the Father, possibly by way of a theophany, a visible manifestation of God the Father. Jesus declared to him, and to the others of the Twelve, John 14:6a, exegeted, "I am the way of salvation into the Kingdom/Recreation, I am the truth of salvation with respect to the Kingdom,/Recreation, and I am the life of salvation in the Kingdom/Recreation." That salvation included knowing the eternally invisible God the Father and possessing the eternally invisible God the Spirit. Since, Jesus in his humanity spoke with the Father's authority and accomplished the Father's works, the Twelve knew God the Father. Jesus' works, which he accomplished through his divinity, revealed God the Father by way of his excellences.

Throughout his ministry, Jesus in his exulting works simultaneously revealed the glory of the Father; for ardently, John 14:6b, "No one comes to the Father except through me." And the only way to the Father came in believing Jesus, the Lord and Savior. In that knowing, Jesus revealed the glory of the Father, John 1:14, as well as the knowledge of the glory of God, 2 Corinthians 4:6. Hence, in his workings, the Christ through his humanity represented also the glory and the wisdom of God the Father, 1 Corinthians 1:24, the eternal life in the Father too, 1 John 1:1–3. And the love Christ Jesus revealed corresponded with the love of the Father, John 3:16; Romans

5:8; 1 John 3:1; etc. Believing Jesus' manifestation of undeserved favor equaled trusting God the Father's unmerited mercy. Consequently, John 14:11, "Believe me that I am in the Father and the Father is in me, or else believe on account of the works themselves." This believing glorified God the Father too, John 12:28.

Hence, as the Father sent the Son, the Son, within the bounds of his ministry, made God the Father known.

Revealing the Father confirmed the work of God the Son. In the revelation of Jesus Christ, God the Spirit informed the Church that God the Father had mapped out the groundplan for the universe, 1 Corinthians 8:6a; Revelation 4:11. On the basis of this original planning, God the Son had summoned forth the created order in its entirety, the whole intent on glorifying the Trinity.

In the revelation of Jesus Christ, God the Spirit pointed out in the Church that God the Father designed the groundwork of salvation—the salvation of his people throughout the first dispensation, the sending of God the Son into Israel, and the Crucifixion. Paul even identified God the Father as the Savior. First Timothy 1:1, 4:10, "For to this end we toil and strive, because we have our hope set on the living God, who is the Savior of all people, especially of those who believe." Now, to know the Father is to know who planned the groundwork of salvation—the eternal, indestructible groundplan. This knowing is Christ Jesus' work as well as God the Spirit's dynamics.

Christ Jesus, by making God the Father known 1) opened windows on the indestructibility of salvation, propitiation, and justification, 2) affirmed the gravitas of the Trinity, and 3) promoted the magnification of the Divinity.

7

At decisive junctions in Jesus' ministry, God the Father exhorted the New Church to listen to her Lord and Savior. So at Jesus' baptism, Matthew 3:17; Mark 1:11; Luke 3:22b, "You are my beloved Son; with you I am wellpleased." God the Spirit by descending on Jesus' humanity affirmed this exhortation.

Another time, on the Mount of Transfiguration, Matthew 17:5; Mark 9:7; Luke 9:35, the Father declared to Peter, James, and John, with reference to Jesus, "This is my beloved Son, my Chosen One; listen to him." Thus God the Father confirmed Jesus in his humanity eternally conjoined to his divinity as the Beloved, whose Gospel all generations have to hear and obey.[16]

---

16. Acts 4:12, "And there is salvation in no one else, for there is no other name under heaven given among men by which we must be saved."

On another occasion, John 12:28b, the Father, responding to Jesus' magnification of his name, declared, "I have glorified it, and I will glorify it again." As Jesus glorified the Father, he willed the New Church to emulate him, wholeheartedly.

At each of these decisive points of reckoning, the Father confirmed Jesus in his divinity and humanity as the Lord and Savior. Flawless, he impressed his voice first and foremost on the Twelve who heard these teachings on the way to Golgotha. Each time, the Father articulated one theme: Listen to Jesus! This intense listening the Apostles uninhibitedly proclaimed to the emerging congregations.

8

The eternal Father created the groundwork relative to pardoning grace. Matthew 6:14–15, "For if you forgive others their trespasses, your heavenly Father will also forgive you, but if you do not forgive others their trespasses, neither will your Father forgive your trespasses." In the Church, God the Father set the clemency-standard—as the faithful forgive, he forgives, the forgiveness perpetuating the Savior's Atonement merited on Golgotha. Exercising this compassionate grace indicates the Church's evidential believing and knowing the forgiveness of sins, thus cleansing her of hates, grudges, and feuds. Jesus enlarged the actualities of clemency in the Parable of the Unforgiving Servant, Matthew 18:21–35. An apostle presented these caring acts of neighborly mercy explicitly. Second Corinthians 7:10,

> For godly grief produces a repentance that leads to salvation without regret, whereas worldly grief produces death.

Simon Peter and Judas Iscariot presented this moving evidence of the Faith, Peter for life, Matthew 26:75b, and Judas for death, Matthew 27:4; Acts 1:18.

9

At times, Jesus, physically, mentally, and emotionally worn and weary of carrying the atonement-burden, sought isolation for prayer, Mark 1:35; Luke 3:21, 5:16, 6:12; etc. Upon a day's exhausting instruction, healing, and feeding of more than 5,000 followers, he required prayer-full seclusion, Matthew 14:23; Mark 6:46; Luke 9:18. For such communion with God the Father, Jesus with Peter, James, and John ascended what became known as the Mount of Transfiguration, Luke 9:29. To achieve this reinvigoration, he did not appeal to his divinity or to God the Spirit; he selected communing with God the Father for inspiring endurance as well as wisdom, then to move ahead in his Cross-bound mission. On another occasion, overcome by human weaknesses, he sought stamina and perseverance from God the Father to meet the holy demands of Israel's redemption; therefore, in the Garden of Gethsemane, Jesus bared his human soul in its agony over the Crucifixion and its hellish agony, Matthew 26:36-46; Mark 14:32-42; Luke 22:39-46. In excruciating anguish while walking to Golgotha, the Man of Sorrows recognized God the Father who had sent him and appealed for human superiority over sin, Satan, death, and hell, an agony of soul also pressed out at another occasion, John 12:27. Then, after the impressively expressive John 17:1-26 prayer, with his humanity's core of steel tempered, he walked on, determined.

At times, Jesus ordered his followers prayerfully to invoke God the Father's name. Matthew 6:5-6, "And when you pray, you must not be like the hypocrites. For they love to stand and pray in the synagogues and at the street corners, that they may be seen by others. Truly, I say to you, they have received their reward. But when you pray, go into your room and shut the door and pray to your Father who is in secret. And your Father who sees in secret will reward you." Here, the Son of God, Savior, curated another of his Father's standard setting requirements for all who believed his messianic goal. For believers to meet basic tenets for praying, he, in the midst of a busy day taught his disciples its vocal rudiments, Luke 11:1-4; Matthew 6:9-3, which later generations recognized as the Lord's Prayer.

Apostle Paul, Romans 8:26-27, acknowledged in appeals to God the Father the work of God the Spirit to evolve heart-voices.

> . . . the Spirit helps us in our weakness. for we do now know what to pray for as we ought, but the Spirit himself intercedes for us with groanings to deep for words. And he who searches hearts knows what is the mind of the Spirit, because the Spirit intercedes for the saints according to the will of God.

All Spirit-powered petitions as well as thanksgivings ascend out of the deeps of believing hearts to the Lord Jesus whose elders store these prayers in golden bowls, forever remembered, Revelation 5:8, 8:3.

10

Also worthy of mention: God the Father broke Peter's stony heart and made the Twelve's spokesman confess Jesus' messiahship. Mark 8:29; Luke 9:20;

Matthew 16:16, "You are the Son of the living God." Thus the disciple/apostle acknowledged Jesus the Lord and Savior.

11

Calling the elect to life and bypassing the reprobate in death originates with God the Father. And Jesus implemented this conceived-in-eternity factuality. Luke 10:21-22; Matthew 11:25-27,

> I thank you, Father, Lord of heaven and earth, that you have hidden [election and reprobation] from the wise and understanding and revealed them to little children; yes, Father, for such was your gracious will. All things have been handed over to me by my Father, and no one knows the Son except the Father, and no one knows the Father except the Son and anyone to whom the Son chooses to reveal him.

Thus the Lord and Savior recognized God the Father for originating before all ages the certainties of predestination to separate the human race into sheep and goats. The latter he bypassed.

Apostle Paul with insightful scriptural wisdom elaborated on this teaching. Romans 8:28-30,

> ... we know that for those who love God all things work together for good, for those who are called according to his purpose. For those whom he foreknew he also predestined to be conformed to the image of his Son, in order that he might be the firstborn among many brothers. And those whom he predestined he also called, and those whom he called he also justified, and those whom he justified he also glorified.

Moreover, the Apostle declared God the Father's rudimentary predestinarian work centered in God the Son. Ephesians 1:4-6,

> Blessed be the God and Father of our Lord Jesus Christ, who has blessed us in Christ with every spiritual blessing in the heavenly places, even as he chose us in him before the foundation of the world, that we should be holy and blameless before him. In love he predestined us for adoption as sons through Jesus Christ, according to the purpose of his will, to the praise of his glorious grace, with which he has blessed us in the Beloved.

In 2 Timothy 1:9-10, Paul once more verified the assurance of election. "[. . . the Father] saved us and called us to a holy calling, not because of our works but because of his own purpose and grace, which he gave us in Christ Jesus before the ages began, and which now has been manifested through the appearing of our Savior Christ Jesus, who abolished death and brought life and immortality to light through the gospel." Second Thessalonians 2:13-14.

Apostle John, similarly informed, recorded that the source of election occurred in eternity. Jesus in prayer, John 17:6a, "I have manifested your name to the people whom you gave me out of the world." These out of Israel formed the first of the forever symbolized 144,000 of Revelation 7:14, 14:1-3, the elect rooted deep in Deuteronomy 7:6-8. "For you are a people holy to the LORD your God. The LORD your God has chosen you to be a people for his treasured possession, out of all the peoples who are on the face of the earth. It was not because you were more in number than any other people that the LORD set his love on you and chose you, for you were the fewest of all peoples, but it is because the LORD loves you and is keeping the oath he swore to your fathers, that the LORD has brought you out with a mighty hand and redeemed you from the house of slavery, from the hand of Pharaoh king of Egypt."[17] All assurances of the foreknowing Father solidified in the love the Lord Jesus Christ manifested.

God the Father from out of eternity, foreknew all creatives whom he with God the Son and the Holy Spirit drew generation upon generation across time together as the Church, unchangeably. Jesus presented this teaching figuratively. Matthew 15:13, "Every plant that my Father has not planted will be rooted up." The Father's works of predestination become inevitably true, the Church actuating this irreversible teaching, 2 Peter 1:10.

12

Salvation on account of election gravitated through faith into eternal life, a dominating theme in the Fourth Gospel. John 3:36a, "Whoever believes in the Son has eternal life." John 4:36, 6:27, 40, "For this is the will of my Father, that everyone who looks on the Son and believes in him should have eternal life, and I will raise him up on the last day." John 6:47, 51, 8:12, 10:28, "I give them eternal life, and they will never perish, and no one will snatch them out of my hand." John 12:50, 17:3, "And this is eternal life, that they know you the only true God, and Jesus Christ whom you have sent." Hence, the elect believing and living the Gospel live eternally.

---

17. Paul in Romans 9-11 expanded on Israel's election under the theme: not all Israel is Israel.

Now, to know the indestructible and unmovable groundwork of the invisible God the Father creates the first evidence of the trinitarian faith. This is to say, unequivocally, to believe God the Father's groundwork for the Kingdom/Recreation and electing the Church solidifies the Faith in eternity.

The Son of God's Exaltation and Humiliation

With the Incarnation, the eternal fusion of Jesus' divinity and humanity—never divinizing his humanity and never humanizing his divinity—God the Son inspired his humanity to suffer the way of the Atonement. The Man of Sorrows in his humanity gained submission through suffering. Hebrew 5:8, "Although he was a son, he learned obedience through what he suffered." In this humiliating process, Jesus submitted heart, mind, and body to extremes of rejection, in the end to agonies beyond agony. Throughout his living, he manifested omnipotence and omniscience, simultaneously absorbing in his humanity punishing burdens of human guilt.

On account of his divinity and humanity, Jesus knew exaltation and humiliation, the latter with the Incarnation, suffering, crucifixion, death, and burial, the former in his works, resurrection, ascension, and session, that is, ruling heaven and earth at the right hand of God the Father.

To know Jesus in his multiple works is to know God the Father in his foundation-laying groundwork with respect to the Kingdom/Recreation and the salvation of the Church.

Jesus' Exaltation

According to his exalted and exulting divinity, Jesus appeared in Israel the equal of God the Father and God the Spirit. On earth and in Israel, the Lord Jesus through his workings revealed laudable criteria, each astonishing in authority—John 5:17, 10:30, 14:9b; Colossians 1:15, 2:9; Hebrews 1:3; etc. In short, during his ministry, he magnified his divinity in his humanity to glorify God the Father and God the Spirit in the erection of the Kingdom/Recreation.

Identity Criteria

Scriptures' Author/authors revealed Jesus' joys in his eternally bonded humanity/divinity: he recognized himself the Christ. From out of the unity of his being, he plainly stated the salvation in his name, his humanity every step of the way sacrificially involved. This is to say, his humanity was not a conduit for his divinity; both identified his being relative to the final transformation of the Kingdom/Recreation. For this historical rule, his humanity rejoiced with splendors of holiness.

1

At Jesus' revelations of full equivalency with God the Father and God the Spirit, many Israelites, transitorily, gloried in his celestial authority.

    Matthew 14:33, "Truly, you are the Son of God."

    Matthew 15:31b, "And they glorified the God of Israel."

    Mark 2:12b, "We never saw anything like this!"

    John 1:14b, ". . . glory as of the only Son from the Father, full of grace and truth."

    John 12:13p, "Blessed is he who comes in the name of the Lord, even the King of Israel!"

    And John 20:28, Thomas, "My Lord and my God!"

To just acclaim, the glory of divinity intimately involved and reflected from Jesus' physical works, each magnifying the Trinity.

Jesus exalted in his equality with God the Father's "I am," Exodus 3:14. Therefore, by opening his own "I am," Isaiah 43:10, Mark 14:62, to the New Testament Author/authors, he revealed his incarnational joys most aptly.

    John 6:35, "I am the bread of life."

    John 8:12, "I am the light of the world."

    John 8:24, "I told you that you would die in your sins, for unless you believe that I am he you will die in your sins."

    John 8:58, ". . . I say to you, before Abraham was, I am."

    John 9:5, "As long as I am in [Israel], I am the light of [Israel]."

    John 10:7, "I am the door of the sheep."

    John 10:11a, "I am the good shepherd."

    John 11:25a, "I am the resurrection and the life."

    John 13:19b, ". . . that when it does take place you may believe that I am he."

TRINITARIAN EXALTATION

John 14:6a, "I am the way, and the truth, and the life."

John 15:1a "I am the true vine."

John 18:5a, "I am he."

Such sayings, expressive of Jesus' humanity, accentuated his divine omnipotence and omniscience. Hence, in many ways through this physicality, he declared the reality of his eternal existence, John 3:13, 6:33, 38, 46, 62; etc. Definitely and effectively, his divinity bonded to his servant-humanity highlighted these excellences.

As in heaven, also on earth: according to Fourth Gospel, conspicuously, God the Father exulted in the Son's ministry. John 8:54, 13:31–32, 16:14, "He will glorify me, for he will take what is mine and declare it to you." John 17:1b–2, "Father, the hour has come; glorify your Son that the Son may glorify you, since you have given him authority over all flesh, to give eternal life to all whom you have given him." God the Father thus rejoiced in Jesus' ministry—even when waves of hatred submerged him in death.

2

In the face of death, as church leaders plotted murder, Christ Jesus amplified his divinity. Matthew 9:1–8; Mark 2:1–12; Luke 5:17–26; etc. With his humanity at stake, he gloried in irreversible incarnational joys.

Apostle John too stressed the impetus of this murderous crudity roiling about in Israel's heart. When Jesus announced his equality with God the Father, the Jews conspired against him. John 5:18,

> This was why the Jews were seeking all the more to kill him, because not only was he breaking the Sabbath, but he was even calling God his own Father, making himself equal with God.

John 10:20, 31, 39, 11:53 left no doubt about Jewish intentions; they wanted the Messiah dead and all evidence of the Incarnation erased.

Blind to Jesus' divinity, they attacked his visible humanity. As his divinity resolutely engaged his humanity, in his humanity he acknowledged dependence on God the Father's groundplan for the coming of the Kingdom/Recreation and the Church's salvation; from the Father, he acquired physical and mental strengths of willpower for the judicious acts of implementing the salvific blueprint. Even with the nearing crucifixion, the joys of the Incarnation shone; he had come for implementing in his humanity the re-founding of the Kingdom/Recreation—to which Israel was blind.

3

Apostle John, 5:19–24, adroitly registered coherent joys Jesus had revealed:

Joy one. "Truly, truly, I say to you, the Son can do nothing of his own accord, but only what he sees the Father doing. For whatever the Father does, that the Son does likewise." To accomplish the groundplan, the Father inspired the Son in his humanity.

Joy two. "For the Father loves the Son and shows him all that he himself is doing." And since God the Father and God the Spirit willed working through God the Son's humanity to actualize the grace of salvation, all whom the Father gave him came and come into the light. "And greater works than these will [the Father] show him, so that [even nasty church leaders] may marvel." In the servanthood of his humanity, Jesus structured the Gospel and presented to the Father the implemented Kingdom/Recreation.

Joy three. "For as the Father raises the dead and gives them life, so also the Son (with his humanity) gives life to whom he will." This resurrection of believers out of the death of unbelief motivated the Son to reach eschatologically ahead.

Joy four. "The Father judges no one, but has given all judgment to the Son, that all may honor the Son, just as they honor the Father." Jesus, according to his divinity, strove omnisciently in his humanity to move historical events into the first and great Judgment, making the dividing-line apparent. "Whoever does not honor the Son (through his humanity) does not honor the Father who sent him."

Joy five. "Truly, truly, I say to you, whoever hears my word and believes him who sent me has eternal life. He does not come into judgment, but has passed from death to life." This judgment, the Crucifixion, that is, the final Passover, Jesus clarified. Reminiscent of Daniel 12:2, John 5:25–29,

> Truly, truly, I say to you, an hour is coming, and now is here, when the dead will hear the voice of the Son of God, and those who hear will live. For as the Father has life in himself, so he has granted the Son also to have life in himself. And he has given him authority to execute judgment, because he is the Son of Man. Do not marvel at this, for an hour is coming when all who are in the tombs will hear his voice and come out,[18] those who have done good to the resurrection of life, and those who have done evil to the resurrection of judgment.

---

18. Earlier, Matthew, 27:51–53, previewed this resurrection; for a number of people came to life, to die again.

As the incarnate Son in his humanity and divinity accomplished the Father's groundwork in regard to the Kingdom/Recreation, he rejoiced the more. John 5:30, "I can do nothing on my own. As I hear, I judge, and my judgment is just, because I seek not my own but the will of him who sent me." As the enmitous clutches of evil enclosed about him, Jesus called on the Father's witness to strengthen him in his humanity for the goal of the Incarnation.

After nourishing the 5,000, John 6:1–15, as nastier Pharisaic spirits viciously threatened death, Jesus in the joy of the Incarnation presented his body and blood as the food and drink for eternal life. John 6:32b, ". . . my Father gives you the true bread from heaven. For the bread of God is he who comes down from heaven and gives life to [Israel]." He thereby declared his humanity's full import. John 6:53–55,

> Truly, truly, I say to you, unless you eat the flesh of the Son of Man and drink his blood, you have no life in you. Whoever feeds on my flesh and drinks my blood has eternal life, and I will raise him up on the last day. For my flesh is true food, and my blood is true drink.

Therewith Jesus in his humanity revealed the incarnational joys at calling and gathering a people for the Kingdom/Recreation.

Naming Criteria

The early Church, setting the standard for following generations, knew Jesus according to multiple names;[19] each one gloriously reflected and reflects his majestic sovereignty in all the earth, indeed, over the entire universe.

He is Jesus, Matthew 1:21, ". . . for he will save his people from their sins."
He is God the Almighty, Revelation 15:3.
He is the Word[20] and the Word of God, John 1:1.
He is the Word of life, 1 John 1:1–2.
He is the Lamb, John 1:29; Revelation 5:6.
He is the Lion of Judah, Revelation 5:5.
He is the Root of David, Revelation 5:5.
He is the Christ, the Messiah, Matthew 16:16, 20; Mark 8:29; Luke 9:20.
He is the Son of David, Matthew 1:1; Mark 12:35; Luke 20:41.

---

19. This naming represents no particular order; collectively, the listing indicates the Incarnate's vitality in divinity and humanity.

20. Rather than immersing Christianity in Greek philosophy, the Johannine Logos exudes Hebrew thinking, Isaiah 2:3, 38:4, 6, 55:11; Revelation 19:13; etc.

He is the Son of God, Matthew 4:3, 8:29, 8:29, 14:32; Luke 1:35; Acts 9:20.
He is the Son of the living God, Matthew 16:16.
He is the Son of the Most High God, Mark 5:7; Luke 8:28.
He is the Son of Abraham, Matthew 1:1.
He is the Creator of angels, Colossians 1:16.
He is the King of the Jews, Matthew 2:2, 25:34, 40.
He is the King of Israel, Zechariah 9:9/Matthew 27:26.
He is Jesus of Nazareth, the Nazarene, Matthew 2:23, 21:11.
He is the God of Israel, Matthew 15:31.
He is the Light of the world, John 8:12.
He is the Lord, Matthew 22:45; Mark 12:37.
He is the God of Abraham, Isaac, and Jacob, Matthew 22:32; Mark 12:26.
He is the Immanuel, Isaiah 7:14/Matthew 1:23.
He is the Son of Man, Matthew 8:20, 26:64; Mark 2:10, 14:62; Luke 5:24, 22:69.
He is the First and the Last, Isaiah 44:6, 41:4/Revelation 1:8, 17, 21:6.
He is the King of kings and Lord of lords, Revelation 19:16.
He is the "I am," John 6:41, 10:9.
He is the Holy One of God, John 6:69.
He is the Wisdom of God, Luke 11:49.
He is Christ Jesus, Acts 17:3.
He is the Amen, Revelation 3:14.
He is God, 1 John 5:20.
Etc.[21]

With varying weights of respect, he was also called Teacher/Rabbi, Matthew 8:19, 12:38, 19:16; Mark 10:17; Luke 18:18; Matthew 22:16, 36; Mark 12:14; Luke 20:21; Matthew 22:24; Mark 12:19; Luke 20:28; Mark 12:19; Matthew 26:49;[22] Mark 12:32, even Rabboni, John 20:16.

Distinct from names for God the Father and God the Spirit, Jesus' many New Testament identifiers served and serve to intensify the Church's magnification: he is the Lord and the Savior. These names, however, individually or even collectively, cannot contain the totality of his regal authority over the Kingdom/Recreation.

---

21. Anatolios. *Retrieving Nicaea*, 112, "Since the Scriptures as a whole (and for that matter all facets of Christian life) assert the unique preeminence of Christ, that preeminence must be applied to the interpretation of all of the Christological titles in a way that maximizes their value to the point of associating him with the very being of God."

22. According to the RSV, the forever beguiled Judas Iscariot called Jesus "master."

Providential Criteria

The Christ governs all weather patterns; from horrendous tempests to gentlest summer breezes, with his sovereignty he mobilizes meteorological elements; these workings he rooted deeply in the Old Testament dispensation.

1

> The heavens declare the glory of God,
> and the sky above proclaims his handiwork.
> Psalm 19:1

Upon creating heaven and earth, the LORD God also initiated his providential rule, separating land from water and turning the seasons. Basic to all weather patterns lay the LORD God's assurance of seasonal cyclicality, Genesis 8:20–22. The Climate-changer inspired the Psalmist, 107:25, to deep-hearted acclaim:

> For he commanded and raised the stormy wind,
> which lifted up the waves of the sea.

2

Out of his omnipotence and omniscience, the omnipresent LORD God began and ended the Noahic Flood, Genesis 7:17–24, 8:1–5. He brought about droughts/famines, Genesis 12:10, 26:1, 41:53–55. For the Exodus, 14:21, the LORD drove back the Red Sea waters with a strong east wind. He promised Israel the early and the late rains, Deuteronomy 11:14. Nehemiah affirmed that the LORD God's universal rule served as the base for Israel's history, 9:6, "You are the LORD, you alone. You have made heaven, the heaven of heavens, with all their host, the earth, and all that is on it, the seas and all that is in them, and you preserve all of them; and the host of heaven worships you." Wide-ranging Psalm 148 too magnifies his universal dominion.

> Praise him, sun and moon,
> praise him, all you shining stars!
> Praise him, you highest heavens,
> and you waters above the heavens!

Despite Adam's cataclysmic fall, the God of gods preserved and sustained the entirety of his creation, Israel his evidence. He even brought on the storm that compelled Jonah, 1:4, to complete his mission. He also sent Jonah, 4:8, a "sultry east wind" to humble the vengeful man.

3

Testing the ambivalent Twelve and proving his saving authority, he unchained and restrained storms, one of which recounted in Mark 4:35–41; Luke 8:22–25; Matthew 8:24. "And behold, there arose a great storm on the sea, so that the boat was being swamped by the waves; but he was asleep." Through his inviolable divinity, the Weather-maker managed even the wildest weathers. And again, Matthew 14:22–23; Mark 6:45–52; John 6:16–21. On account of his saving dominion, Jesus made storms come and go.

Because he intended that Paul finish his ministry in Rome, the Apostle survived the weeks-long Northeaster, Acts 27:1–44.

Violent and gentle meteorological fluctuations reflect the Christ's preserving and sustaining authority. More than making the sun rise on the evil and the good and more than sending rain on the just and the unjust, the movements in the created order rest in his omnipotence, omniscience, and omnipresence.

Hence, through Apostle Paul, he asserted the presence of the unshakable Kingdom/Recreation, Colossians 1:17, ". . . he is before all things, and in him all things hold together." The finite universe in its totality of cycling galaxies and spinning neutrons, because the Christ holds it together, provides the Church with the conviction and certitude for maturing in her often inhibiting earthly environment.

The Author/author of the Letter to the Hebrews, 1:3p, too affirms the Christ's sovereignty, namely, ". . . he upholds the universe by the word of his power." All that happens, cosmically, globally, and regionally, occurs at the Son of God's direction while he commands the Church in its Kingdom/Recreation habitat to move on, wholeheartedly magnifying the Trinity, even during illnesses, with handicaps, John 9:3, and earthquakes, Matthew 27:51, 28:2.

The heartening hope the Spirit thus engenders has substance, which the numerous Christian congregations believe amidst even worsening climate changes. Romans 8:19–21, "For the creation waits with eager longing for the revealing of the sons of God. For the creation was subjected to futility, not willingly, but because of him who subjected it, in hope that the creation itself will be set free from its bondage to corruption and obtain the freedom of the glory of the children of God." Hence, from the worst climatic disasters through to the longest sunlit day, Joshua 10:12–13, the whole of the coherent universe acclaims the Christ' rule for the sake of the Church and the Kingdom/Recreation.[23]

Recreational Criteria

Jesus with his inextricably united humanity and divinity seized the throne of his failing and faltering Kingdom/Recreation from the Serpent's grasp to attain its final and eternal glory. He had tied his *holy, holy, holy* glory, Isaiah 6:3, to the Davidic monarchy, which Jesse's son recognized; awash in accountability, David fearfully and prayerfully acknowledged his human limitations, 2 Samuel 7:18–29; 1 Chronicles 17:16–27. Pertinently, Psalm 8:3–4,

> When I look at your heavens,
> the work of your fingers,
> the moon and the stars, which you have set in place,
> what is man that you are mindful of him,
> and the son of man that you care for him?[24]

Seriously, as the splendor of the Jerusalem throne sank in disarray, Jesus transferred the Old Testament monarchy into his own hands, forever reforming and stabilizing the seat of all authority. And in the Eschaton, all shall see him on the great white throne, Revelation 20:11–15, publicly sifting and shifting the peoples to his right and left according to the first and great Judgement, the Crucifixion, Matthew 25:31–46, and then transport the Church into the totally transformed Kingdom/Recreation for eternally magnifying the One-in-Three.

1

For this magnification, Jesus revealed the ultimate of the Incarnation, awaking all Israel to historical prophecies and precedents underfoot; with virginal Mary's pregnancy, God the Father and God the Spirit initiated the final reformation of the Kingdom/Recreation:

> Matthew 4:17, "From that time Jesus began to preach, saying, 'Repent, for the kingdom of heaven is at hand.'"

---

23. Everything changes, also in the created order. The Lord Jesus to this day cycles the seasons with salutary regularity. Within in this regularity, current civilized uses and abuses of minerals aggravates sinful disorders in creation evoking the Romans 8:22 parturition cries of hope.

24. With the "man" and the "son of man" naming, David recognized in the light of the overwhelmingly glorious LORD the limitations of his judicial authority.

> Matthew 4:23, "And [Jesus] went throughout all Galilee . . . proclaiming the gospel of the kingdom and healing every disease and every affliction among the people."
>
> Mathew 6:33p, ". . . seek first the kingdom of God and his righteousness."
>
> Matthew 10:7p, "The kingdom of heaven is at hand."
>
> Mark 1:14–15, ". . . Jesus came into Galilee, proclaiming the gospel of God, and saying, 'The time is fulfilled, and the kingdom of God is at hand; repent and believe in the gospel.'"
>
> Luke 1:33, Gabriel to Mary, ". . . [Jesus] will reign over the house of Jacob forever, and of his kingdom there will be no end."
>
> Luke 4:43, "I must preach the good news of the Kingdom of God to the other towns as well; for I was sent for this purpose."
>
> Luke 11:2; Matthew 6:10p, "Your kingdom come."
>
> John 3:3, ". . . unless one is born again he cannot see the kingdom of God."
>
> Etc.

Irreversibly, the incarnate Lord and Savior, eschatologically moving, reestablished the foundational Kingdom/Recreation in a world interconnected by disfiguring idolatries, at that time onerous Pharisaic/Sadduceic and Roman negations of the future.

2

For the Kingdom/Recreation, Jesus converted select peoples into citizens, each heart-bound to glory in the Divinity.

> Matthew 9:12–13; Mark 2:17, "Those who are well have no need of a physician, but those who are sick. I came not to call the righteous, but sinners."
>
> Luke 19:10, "For the Son of Man came to seek and to save the lost."
>
> John 1:29b, "Behold, the Lamb of God, who takes away the sin of [Israel]!"
>
> John 3:5, "Truly, truly, I say to you, unless one is born of water and the Spirit, he cannot enter the kingdom of God."

John 3:17, "For God did not send his Son into [Israel] to condemn [Israel], but in order that [Israel] might be saved through him."

John 8:31–32, "If you abide in my word, you are truly my disciples, and you will know the truth, and the truth will set you free."

John 8:36, "So if the Son sets you free, you will be free indeed."

John 12:24, "Truly, truly, I say to you, unless a grain of wheat falls into the earth and dies, it remains alone; but if it dies, it bears much fruit."

John 15:2, "Every branch in me that does not bear fruit [the vinedresser] takes away, and every branch that does bear fruit he prunes, that it may bear more fruit."

John 17:20–21, "I do not ask for these only, but also for those who will believe in me through [the apostles'] word, that they may all be one, just as you, Father, are in me, and I in you, that they also may be in us, so that the world may believe that you have sent me."

Etc.

With these and many other praise-full assertions, Jesus willed during his millennial reign that all assigned thereto administer the Kingdom/Recreation; for this administering, he allocates gifts, Romans 12:3–8; 1 Corinthians 12:4–11; 1 Peter 4:10–11, prophesying, serving, teaching, exhorting, contributing, leading, and greatest of all, loving.[25]

3

At recreating his monarchy, the Lord Jesus followed royal protocol; in early days, he dispatched a train of prophets to announce his advent. The last of these spirited heralds, John the Baptizer, honored his mandate by proclaiming the King's imminent arrival. Isaiah 40:3–5; Malachi 3:1; Matthew 3:3; Luke 3:4–6; Mark 1:2–3,

> Behold, I send my messenger before your face,
> who will prepare your way,[26]

---

25. First Corinthians 13:1–13.

26. Matthew, 11:10, and Luke, 7:27, referred to the first line of Isaiah 40:3–4, therewith indicating the whole of this prophecy.

> the voice of one crying in the wilderness:
> "Prepare the way of the Lord,
> make his paths straight."

John' baptism, therefore, served to cleanse and prepare covenant people to encounter the Christ.

Apostle John, in distinction, recorded the Baptizer's significance from more immediate observation. John 1:6–8, 19–28, and 5:33–35. Jesus' calculated rebuke therefore to unhinged ecclesiastics. "You sent to John, and he has borne witness to the truth. Not that the testimony that I receive is from man, but I say these things so that you may be saved. He was a burning and shining lamp, and you were willing to rejoice for a while in his light." At Jesus' baptism, the Baptizer's light shone its brightest.

Alive, the Baptizer faithfully, even boldly, advanced his commission; he proclaimed the imminence of the Kingdom/Recreation and the King. Matthew 3:2, "Repent, for the kingdom of heaven is at hand."[27] With such noble agency, John commanded the obedience of faith, raising all whom God the Father had appointed out of pits of unbelief onto heights of faithfulness. The men he immersed into Jordan waters prepared to welcome Israel's one and only Lord; in fact, by this baptismal rite, all immersed promised to sideline other pressing interests and arrange then-and-there to meet and greet the King.

Again, following royal protocol, Jesus had a procession escort him into Jerusalem. So, in the immediate approach to his coronation, Jesus located a donkey, fulfilling Zechariah 9:9/Matthew 21:1–11; Luke 19:28–44; John 12:12–19. He made the ecstatic procession happen, John 12:15. Even as the butt of swelling Pharisee/Sadducee hatred, Jesus—visibly human, invisibly divine—in all humility pushed on. Amidst euphoric praises from Israel's hopeful and the Sanhedrin's damning polarizers, Jesus rode his beast of burden toward the day of unimaginable suffering and death, all the forces of hell to pounce on his weakened and scourged humanity. Yet, for the redemption of his peoples, Jesus pressed on to his waiting throne, holding high Revelation 19:10p, namely, "For the testimony of Jesus is the spirit of prophecy."

---

27. Matthew preferred the Kingdom-of-Heaven naming, for example, 8:11, 13:33, 44, 45, 47, 52; etc. Mark and Luke worked with the Kingdom-of-God designation, a generic identification, not assuming that this was God the Father's Kingdom, but the realm over which Jesus ruled.

4

To actualize the transfer from Davidides on the Kingdom/Recreation's throne to himself, *the* Davidide, Jesus passed through the crucifixion-hell to the resurrection-glory, and onto the enthronement at the Ascension. To accentuate the factuality of the Kingdom/Recreation, he instituted the Church, Acts 2:42–47, the very epicenter from which throughout the second dispensation he proclaimed his sovereign rule, the first obligation of every Christian congregation.

For ruling the Kingdom/Recreation, Jesus incessantly reformed the face of the earth and redirected the sense of the universe, the whole of the created order daily adjusting to the presence of the Church. Without the Kingdom/Recreation transfiguring world history and the biblical awareness of the universe's final glory—incorporation into the Kingdom/Recreation— the old ways of human domination degrade further into sorry arenas of little gods devastatingly at war with each other, although by the end, Jesus will bend all together for Revelation 16:16's Armageddon. Since the Ascension, he affirms his omnipotent, omniscient, and omnipresent rulership; at the same time he compels the *official opposition* into retreat and defeat.

5

Jesus sent the disciples/apostles into hateful Israel and to ends of the earth, Matthew 10:1–4; Mark 3:13–19; Luke 6:12–16; John 6:70–71, 15:16, 17:18, "As you sent me into [Israel], so I have sent [the Twelve] into the world." This commissioning took hold immediately upon Pentecost. Matthew 28:20–21, "Go therefore and make disciples of all nations, baptizing them in the name of the Father and of the Son and of the Spirit, teaching them to observe all that I have commanded you. And behold, I am with you always, to the end of the age." Luke, 24:49a, to the Twelve, "And behold, I am sending the promise of my Father upon you." And John 20:21? "Peace be with you. As the Father has sent me, even so I am sending you." Paul he sent to work among the Gentiles, Peter in Israel, Acts 9:15; Galatians 2:8. Malleably, Jesus made the duty-bound Twelve carry on where he had left off.[28]

Jesus commissioned the apostles to speak the power of the word into a world ready for harvesting.

---

28. Poythress. *The Mystery of the Trinity,* 21, "By confirming publicly the authenticity of Jesus' claims, the resurrection also shows that the apostles of Jesus are authentic messengers of God who proclaim the true Word of God."

6

So, reigning supremely in the revelation of the Kingdom/Recreation, the Son of God over three years of ministry in Israel disclosed the primary evidence of his supremacy; from day to day he intensified the markers of his authoritative rule.

All such recreative service, however, angered Israel's Sanhedrin; the principal Pharisees and Sadducees, feeding on ambition, feared loss of control over Synagogue and Temple. Hence, with ill-concealed defiance, they barred those immersed in John's baptism from acknowledging the Son of God, John 7:13, 9:22, 12:42, 16:2; out of proliferating truculence, the Pharisee/Sadducee powers reviled Jesus throughout his ministry; relentlessly and murderously, they harassed him.

Israel's rulers, in sharp contrast to Jesus' dominion of grace, fused coercive power upsurges into methodological domineering; this sort of bullying simulated intolerant Egyptian, Assyrian, Babylonian, Grecian, and Roman autocrats, which regimes of punitive repression forced subject peoples into dregs of idolatry. In that situational awareness, the Son of God as the King of kings and Lord of lords contrasted his rulership with that of past and present tyrants. Matthew 20:20–28; Mark 10:42–45,

> And Jesus called [the Twelve] to him and said to them, "You know that those who are considered rulers of the Gentiles lord it over them, and their great ones exercise authority over them. But it shall not be so among you. But whoever would be great among you must be your servant, and whoever would be first among you must be slave of all."[29]

In governing the Kingdom/Recreation, the Son of God revealed the holiness of grace to the living citizens who believed in him, in the Faith glorifying the Trinity.

7

The fraudulent Serpent/Devil had misjudged Eve's Seed,[30] desperately so, by offering him the kingdoms of this world for a simple and painless genuflection, Matthew 4:9; Luke 4:7. The Lord and Savior, God the Son, by virtue of creation owned not merely the earth, but the universe; he even deployed the Serpent's movements and schemes, each of which parted the faithful

---

29. First Peter 5:1–5.
30. Galatians 3:16.

from the unfaithful. In his omnipotence and omniscience, Jesus—divinely conscious of the impending pain—nevertheless in his humanity walked to Golgotha totally aware of the cost to regain maximal dominion over the universe.

Upon Resurrection Day, and more forcefully upon Pentecost Day, Jesus manifested the initial evidence of the Kingdom/Recreation, the Spirit-endowed Church. In his majestic rule, out of nothing he raised the New Testament Church with her multiple congregations of men and women bound to one objective and united in one ambition. Starting in Jerusalem and migrating along Roman roads laid down for imperial dominance, his followers settled in the elsewhere of the Empire, resolutely instituting congregations, therein and wherein to magnify the Trinity and sacrifice themselves to faith, hope, and love; as the Lord and Savior had committed himself, they with many Gentiles whom the Father had chosen for inclusion demonstrated the actuality of Jesus' dominion, such the significance of church membership. Matthew 24:14,

> And this gospel of the kingdom will be proclaimed throughout the whole world as a testimony to all nations, and then the end will come.

In time, Spirit-driven peoples other than Israelites joined themselves to living the Commandments. With international breadth and global width, more believing Gentiles and Israelites with radical solidarity confessed and confess Jesus the King of kings and the Lord of lords, his Kingdom/Recreation reshaping world history, in fact, also renewing awareness of the universe's actual significance.

Legal Criteria

As the Lord of the universe opened the second dispensation, three legal systems competed for primacy—the Decalogue against the Jewish Oral Law and the Roman Law, the Oral Law against the Decalogue and the Roman Law, and the Roman Law against the Oral Law and the Decalogue. In the drawn-out contention, no accommodation or assimilation formed a fourth judiciary satisfactory to adherents of these legal systems.

1

The monotheistic god of the Pharisees/Sadducees *persuaded* his worshipers to gather and obey 613 directives drawn from the Pentateuch called the Oral

Law; this arrangement they then attributed to Moses, John 5:45, 9:28; Romans 2:17; etc. Thus Moses[31] functioned as an iron-clad pillar supporting Pharisaism/Sadduceism. With respect to the Oral Law, in Israel the emerging Pharisees, later joined by the Sadducees, crowded away the Ten Commandments and held the Roman Law at bay. Obsessive obedience to the Oral Law ostensibly merited a chimeric salvation, self-righteousness earned by observing the duplicitous 613 rules of Pharisaic/Sadduceic life.

According to the Tradition of the Elders, invasive religiosity, Matthew 15:1-9; Mark 7:1-8, of which the Oral Law the motivating whip to action, the Jews banked fallacious merits redeemable at death for a counterfeit redemption.

The Pharisees/Sadducees opposed Jesus and the coming of the Kingdom/Recreation; the systematized self-righteousness they invented made the Incarnation not only unnecessary but also enmitous to the Tradition of the Elders. In fact, the repressive Tradition of the Elders nullified the Old Testament prophecies with respect to the Incarnation; by effectively living the Oral Law, the Pharisees/Sadducees easily pleased the god they worshiped. Rather than heartily bow to the Gospel in its Old Testament formulations, those heretics built an alternative legal system by means of which to devise an impossible salvation. With its Trinity-spurning monotheism, the Pharisees/Sadducees bitterly opposed the Christ and the Gospel, in time gathering up polarizing hatred, Matthew 9:3, 12:14; Mark 2:6, 3:6; Luke 5:21, 6:11. Out of this hatred, the Jews demonized Jesus with Beelzebul naming, Matthew 12:22-30; Mark 3:22-27; Luke 11:14-23; John 10:20. This odium permeated the Tradition of the Elders, Matthew 13:53-58; Mark 6:1-6; Luke 4:16-30.

Jesus in calling all Israel to repentance left no stone unturned to expose Jewish hypocrisy as well as heresy, John 7:7, 11:50-53, 15:18, 25; Luke 11:53-54; Matthew 12:9-14. In his inimitable manner, he provoked reaction to expose the reprobation of his Old Church enemies.

Sliding from upper echelons down, loss of money and prestige a constant worry, John 12:11, 19, the Pharisee/Sadducee hierarchy insisted that all Israel, Jesus too, submit to its legalistic rules, therewith to gratify the Jewish god, a deified creature, John 7:30, 8:44, 15:23, 16:1-4; every Israelite had to bow to the living and breathing Serpent, the Satan, poised for a final encounter to prove Genesis 3:14-19 in error and Jesus an intolerable savior. The Devil no longer trusted other idolatrous proxies to prevent the Gospel's efficacy, but himself drove the Pharisees/Sadducees to his divisive hating.

---

31. In John 1:17a, 7:19; etc., Moses stands in for the Oral Law; so, Acts 13:39, "the law of Moses."

For that reason, to motivate the Sanhedrin leaders to the utmost sabotage, he ensconced himself in the Pharisee/Sadducee stronghold, the Tradition of the Elders, the satanic Oral Law serving to spread utmost derision for Jesus and the eternal manifestation of the Kingdom/Recreation. Retaliatory, Pharisaism/Sadduceism fatally repelled the Son of Man.

Jews attempted to trap Jesus in dispute over Roman taxes, Luke 20:19-26; Matthew 22:15-22; Mark 12:13-17. Had Jesus endorsed Caesarian taxation, he lost credibility among his own people. Had he disallowed the Roman tax, he troubled tax-hungry Roman authorities.

The Lord and Savior's key confrontation with the Roman authorities happened through Pharisee/Sadducee collusion; in the dark of night, a mob armed with swords and clubs arrested him. The Sanhedrin wanted him dead on a charge of blasphemy, Matthew 26:65-66; Mark 14:63-64; Luke 23:70-71; John 18:19-24. John 19:7-8, "We have a law,[32] and according to that law he ought to die because he has made himself the Son of God." According to Mark 15:12-14, Pontius Pilate twice demanded, "What evil has he done?" According to Luke, 23:4, 14, 22, the governor found Jesus blameless of machinations against the Empire. Herod, the Tetrarch of Galilee, corroborated his judgment, Luke 23:6-16. In the trial proceedings, upon investigation, Pilate found no criminal activity in Jesus, John 19:6.

Only, when the Jews entered into the proceedings evidence of Jesus' kingship did Pilate bow to the Sanhedrin's drastic remedy; residual fears of anti-Caesarism sprang to life, John 18:37. For the governor interpreted the Son-of-God naming as anti-Caesarian, which fears the Jews inflamed. John 19:12-13, "If you release this man, you are not Caesar's friend. Everyone who makes himself a king opposes Caesar." Luke 23:23-25,

> ... they were urgent, demanding with loud cries that he should be crucified. And their voices prevailed. So Pilate decided that their demand should be granted. He released [Barabbas] who had been thrown in prison for insurrection and murder, for whom they asked, but he delivered Jesus over to their will.

Unsettled by fears of losing his governorship, Pilate yielded the Son of Man to the excruciating Roman death; to rid himself of an early morning frustration, the governor, indifferent, washed his hands of culpability in wrongfully committing this bloodied and battered Jew to death, Matthew 27:24-26.

Roman Law, as the Oral, served the satanic impulse to crush the Lord and Savior. A squad of Roman soldiers, "lawless men," Acts 2:23, executed

---

32. Oral Law #3, based on Exodus 22:28; Leviticus 24:16a, "Whoever blasphemes the name of the LORD shall surely be put to death." See: "A List of the 613 Mitzvot (Commandments)" at www.jewfag.org/toc.hcam.

Jesus. Thereupon Pontius Pilate and Roman Law lost interest in one more dead Jew.

With the Crucifixion, however, the Roman Empire, representative of the world, arrived at its major reason for existence; in the centuries beyond the Resurrection, over a slow timeline, the Empire disintegrated. As the Empire, decrepit in old age, fragmented and collapsed, Jesus grew the Kingdom/Recreation and defeated efforts to damage its growth.

Because of its biblical misinterpretation, because of its man-made righteousness, and because of its satanic orientation, Jesus condemned the Tradition of the Elders and spurned this misleading religiosity, the whole a bedeviled fabrication incapable of the Decalogue's righteous imperatives.

With Jesus' Cross-death, the Old Church's relevance had run its course. Afterwards, upon the Resurrection/Ascension, the Lord and Savior pushed Judaism aside, a religiosity apart.

Still, Jesus drew some Pharisee-hearted into the New Israel to define the abyss between the grace of the Gospel and the works-righteousness demanded by the Oral Law. By stirring up contentions, Circumcision Party affiliates insisted that Gentile men validate the Faith by the circumcision cut, thereby refuting the perfection of grace. Hence, the Circumcision Party nullified the unearned mercy defined by the Gospel.

Out of this mentality, some faulted Apostle Peter for table fellowship with uncircumcised believers, Acts 11:2–3. To reestablish self-righteousness in the Church, these hypocrites moved to attack in Pisidian Antioch, Acts 13:50, and in Iconium, Acts 14:2. A clash between Circumcision Party associates and Apostle Paul broke the Syrian Antioch congregation apart, Acts 15:1, 5. And all such Party members preserved the "dividing wall of hostility" Jesus had demolished, Ephesians 2:14. They insisted that Gentile believers commit to obeying the high-sounding Oral Law and the nullification of grace. In Jerusalem, they attacked Paul directly and murderously, Acts 21:27. In Galatians 2:11–14, Paul concisely related the crux of the Pharisee/Christian contention. And, in the end, he invoked Isaiah 6:9–10, thereby directing Pharisaism/Sadduceism out of the Church to enter upon its own journey. Acts 18:6, 28:26–27,

> Go to this people,
> and say,
> "You will indeed hear but never understand,
> and you will indeed see but never perceive.
> For this people's heart has grown dull,
> and with their ears they can barely hear,
> and their eyes they have closed;
> lest they should see with their eyes and hear with their ears

> and understand with their heart and turn,
> and I would heal them."

The inspiring Acts of the Apostles thus reveal the Church's progressing missionary history in the Empire. By this time, the Church's missionary work had moved into predominantly Gentile worlds. And that movement became Paul's answer to Jewish intransigence. Concentrating on the synagogue in Rome, he condemned Judaism, hither another religiosity. And the Church in her missionary work found all designated for the Faith, Acts 13:47-48.

Still, the Pharisaic spirit haunted the emerging congregations, unwilling to go away and die.

In the Church at Rome, a Circumcision-Party mentality insisted on the Oral Law in addition to the Gospel. To this Apostle Paul responded, saying, Romans 2:25-29, "For circumcision indeed is of value if you obey . . . law, but if you break . . . law, your circumcision becomes uncircumcision.[33] So, if a man who is uncircumcised keeps the precepts of the law, will not his uncircumcision be regarded as circumcision? Then he who is physically uncircumcised but keeps the law will condemn you who have the written code and circumcision but break the law. For no one is a Jew who is merely one outwardly, nor is circumcision outward and physical. But a Jew is one inwardly and circumcision is a matter of the heart, by the Spirit, not by the letter.[34] His praise is not from man but from God." The Apostle made the separation between the Religion and Pharisaism acutely severe.

In the Corinthian Church, Jewish mob action, Acts 18:12-13, and Pharisaic "super-apostles" aggravated the unity of the congregation and frustrated Paul, 2 Corinthians 11:5.

In the Galatian Churches, muscular remnants of Pharisaism troubled the membership. Galatians 2:15-16, "We ourselves are Jews by birth and not Gentile sinners; yet we know that a person is not justified by works of . . . law but through faith in Jesus Christ, so we also have believed in Christ Jesus, in order to be justified by faith in Christ and not by works of . . . law, because by works of . . . law no one will be justified." Christianity and the Tradition of the Elders never fused; the Religion and any religiosity diverge, the Way from idolatrous ways.

In the Church at Ephesus, various members clung to the reactionary Pharisee-identity and troubled Paul, Acts 20:19, and Timothy too, 1 Timothy 1:3-7, 4:1-5, 6:3-5; 2 Timothy 2:23. Specifically now Ephesians

---

33. Elisions indicate the absence of definite articles, which refer 1) to the Oral Law, alias the written code, and 2) to any idolatrous legal system. In effect, this equates Pharisaism/Sadduceism with other idolatries.

34. Deuteronomy 10:16.

2:14–16, "For [Jesus] himself is our peace, who has made us both [Jews and Gentiles] one and has broken down in his flesh the dividing wall of hostility by abolishing . . . law of commandments expressed in ordinances, that he might create in himself one new man in place of the two, so making peace, and might reconcile us both to God in one body through the cross, thereby killing the hostility." Whereas Jesus had liberated the New Church from the shackling Oral Law, Circumcision-Party agitators sought to hang onto outdated Tradition-of-the-Elders' commitments.

In the Church at Philippi, leaders still commended the Oral Law and sought to imprison members out of the Gentiles in local synagogues. Philippians 3:2–3, "Look out for the dogs, look out for the evildoers, look out for those who mutilate the flesh. For we are the circumcision, who worship by the Spirit of God and glory in Christ Jesus and put no confidence in the flesh." In fact, the Lord and Savior of the Church through Apostle Paul erected the dividing-line between the New Church and the Synagogue.

In the Church at Colossae, 2:4, 16–19, 20–23, Paul, an angel of the Christ, made the blockage between the past of the Synagogue and the future of the Church a matter of life and death. "If with Christ you died to the elemental spirits of the world, why, as if you were still alive in the world, do you submit to regulations—'Do not handle, Do not taste, Do not touch' (referring to things that all perish as they are used)—according to human precepts and teachings? These have indeed an appearance of wisdom in promoting self-made religion and asceticism and severity to the body, but they are of no value in stopping the indulgence of the flesh." Christ Jesus commanded freedom from all impositions of self-righteousness advocated by continuing Jewish religiosity.

The Church at Thessalonica suffered Jewish impositions. First Thessalonians 2:14–16, "For you, brothers, became imitators of the churches of God in Christ Jesus that are in Judea. For you suffered the same things from your own countrymen as they did from the Jews, who killed both the Lord Jesus and the prophets, and drove us out, and displease God and oppose all mankind by hindering us from speaking to the Gentiles that they might be saved—so as always to fill up the measure of their sins. But God's wrath has come upon them at last!" How strong now the distinction between the Church and the Tradition of the Elders!

In the Church on Cyprus, the Circumcision Party mired Titus in Pharisaism, Titus 1:10–11.

The congregations addressed by the Letter to the Hebrews before AD 70 faced the allure of the Temple, Hebrews 2:1–4; they were swayed to reengage with the long familiar feasts and sacrifices, now obsolete. By his sacrifice, Christ Jesus completed all promises inherent in the Temple's sacrificial rites, notably the Passover, purging this building complex of its traditional values. The Church in commemorating the Sacrifice entered every tomorrow.

In the Church at Smyrna nestled a synagogue of Satan to prevent the Faith, Revelation 2:8–11.

In the Church at Pergamum, Satan had made a home to entice commitment to the Oral Law and self-righteousness. Even Nicolaitans were tolerated. Revelation 2:12–17.

In the Church at Thyatira, a Jezebel led members astray in the deep things of Satan, Revelation 2:18–29.

In the Church at Philadelphia members had formed a synagogue of Satan, Revelation 3:7–13.

Over time, the Lord Jesus dispersed and isolated the Jewish synagogual religiosity. Nonetheless, the spirit of legalism lived on in the congregations of the New Church; by adding to or taking from the Gospel, legalists sought control over access to salvation.

2

Rome's pantheon, a fantastic fabulation, swayed the Empire to honor the *pax Romana;* by pleasing these many gods and goddesses, one at a time through opulent festivals, all Roman-hearted strove for the Caesar's peace.

At the turning of the millennia, when the Lord of all the earth irreversibly rotated BC into AD, he had the Empire bestride the known world. This callously cruel Empire, symbolized by Daniel's abhorrent fourth ferocity, 7:7–8, built a relatively harmonious stability and overall prosperity, along with well-maintained road systems. While the Empire gleamed with powers of pride, Jesus compelled this Serpent's proxy with its enormous authority to serve and protect the Kingdom/Recreation.

Consider the Roman Empire a vast forest; within its overbearing shadows, Christ Jesus resuscitated the Davidic rule, the Kingdom/Recreation, as a shoot rooted in rocky Canaan. Post-Ascension, Jesus from his place of authority at the right hand of God the Father, tended this grace-grown sapling springing up out of the dying Isaiah 11:1 Jesse-stump. Simultaneously, he governed the Roman forest, to prevent its towering trees from blocking the sun over the new-growth Kingdom/Recreation. Even as he managed the universe and governed the Roman Empire, Jesus above all graced the one tree.

The Roman monolith owned and operated a ponderous legal system, ostensibly to glorify cumbersome pantheonic inventions; actually these insatiable gods and goddesses *lived* to serve all controlling the Empire, the

Caesars foremost. Rome's legal system protected Rome's pantheon as well as enforced Caesarism, which positioned the idolatrous rulers against *the* King of kings. On occasion, never by happenstance, branches of the grace-tree brushed against the Empire's overshadowing forest monarchs.

Fear of dethronement persuaded Herod the Great, Roman appointee, to seek newborn Jesus' death, Matthew 2:16–18, evoking clamorous lament for wantonly slain lads.

Jesus once spurned Herod the Tetrarch who sought to slay him; to that urge to kill, Jesus singularly responded. Luke 13:32, "Go and tell that fox, 'Behold, I cast out demons and perform cures today and tomorrow, and the third day I finish my course.'" The Son of God intended to die by crucifixion on the appointed day, not an hour sooner.

Upon Pentecost Day, as Jesus gradually grew the Kingdom/Recreation through creating believers and incorporating congregations, each of which identified his rulership. Members of the Jerusalem Church fled the City of the great King, Acts 8:1, and settled at Roman crossroads, every congregation a mission post. To set the pace and start the missionary task among the Gentiles—breaking down the dividing wall of Pharisee/Sadducee hostility—the Lord and Savior summoned Apostle Peter to the home base of a Roman Centurion, Cornelius; there, while the Apostle addressed the household with the Gospel, Acts 10:44–45, ". . . the Holy Spirit fell on all who heard the word. And the believers from among the circumcised who had come with Peter were amazed, because the gift of the Holy Spirit was poured out even on the Gentiles." Upon hearing Peter's account of this deep salvific experience, the leaders and members of the Jerusalem congregation glorified the Christ, acknowledging, Acts 11:18p, "Then to the Gentiles also God has granted repentance that leads to life." By breaking out of the insufferable Pharisee/Sadducee enclosure, the Lord Jesus guided the Church into the uncircumcised world.

Over the first years, other contacts followed—some less than cordial. Philip, Acts 8:4–8, and after him Peter and John, Acts 8:14–25, evangelized in Samaria. Because of such ministry even despised Samaritans received the Holy Spirit and believed the Gospel. Then Philip's encounter with the Ethiopian eunuch, Acts 8:26–40, spread the word of salvation into a foreign country. Herod (the King) to assist the Jews in preventing the progress of the Church beheaded Apostle James and intended the same for Peter, Acts 12:1–5. Moving farther afield, the Cretan governor, Sergius Paulus, believed Barnabas and Paul at the proclamation of the Gospel, Acts 13:4–12. The Philippian jailer and family heard the word of salvation from Paul and Silas; these Gentiles too received the Holy Spirit in measures equal to the charter members of the New Testament Church, Acts 16:25–34. Paul, addressing

Athenian Epicurean and Stoic thinkers, found concretizing resistance to the Faith and only few proselytes. To the philosophers of the Areopagus, he explicated the meaning of the altar to the unknown god, but the vindictive majority mocked the actuality of the Resurrection, Acts 17:22-34. Yet, the believers with the apostles quickened the missionary work, finding all designated for the Faith. Corinthian Jewish authorities attacked Paul and dragged him before the Roman judiciary, but the proconsul, Gallio, refused to consider matters pertaining to the synagogual law, Acts 18:12-16. In Ephesus, Artemus-worshipers rioted against the Way; only, the town clerk quieted the mob and declared his court open only to actual abuse of intermingling Roman religiosities, Acts 19:21-41. Paul, in Jerusalem, seeking to fulfil a vow, was arrested and to prevent suicide by mob action, Acts 21:27-36, had to make an appeal to Caesar, Acts 25:11.

On the whole, Roman authorities cared little for the Kingdom/Recreation. Assured of the Empire's might and the good will of its pantheon, they disregarded the Christ-tree, which grew quietly; more citizens exercised more Trinity-magnifying works. Paul's Romans 13:1-7 and Peter's 1 Peter 2:17p commanded submission to the authorities. The citizens of the Kingdom easily discriminated between obeying God and man, accepting whatever damages civil disobedience incurred. The various levels of Roman government, as Jesus controlled its interests, hardly paid attention of Church and therefore even less to the Kingdom/Recreation. The people of the Church, meanwhile, burdened still by Pharisaic/Sadduceic *kosher* values when associating with Gentiles, listened to Paul, Romans 14:13-23; 1 Corinthians 8:1-13; love for the congregational weaker had to dominate in questions of eating meat first offered to idols and then placed before them at events of Gentile hospitality, 1 Corinthians 10:1-4. Further, Paul and Peter willed that believers maintain fashionable female modesty, 1 Corinthians 11:1-16; 1 Peter 3:1-6. And never to submit to idols, Ephesians 6:10-20; Colossians 1:16; 1 John 5:21.

In time, the Roman Law too had to move aside and make way for the Kingdom/Recreation's Decalogue.

3

The Christ from Mount Sinai's fiery heights revealed the culture-generating Decalogue, the basic legal structure for thanksgiving upon Israel's Exodus salvation. The Ten Commandments outlined the explicit way of gratitude for all serving the LORD God, Yahweh, initially while traversing through the wilderness between Egypt and Canaan.

Jesus by means of his omniscience and through his human way of speaking, the two perfectly coordinated, upheld the Decalogue as the forever valid law of the Kingdom/Recreation. At the beginning of his ministry, then, he explicated the way of decalogual interpretations and demonstrated the superficiality of Pharisee/Sadducee legalism. By exegesis, he revealed the relevance of the Commandments. Whereas the adherents of the Oral Law relied on trivial semblances of righteousness, self-righteousness, the Exegete exposed the inner sanity typical of the Commandments. Matthew 5:17–20,

> Do not think that I have come to abolish the Law or the Prophets; I have not come to abolish them but to fulfill them. For truly, I say to you, until heaven and earth pass away, not an iota, not a dot, will pass from the Law until all is accomplished. Therefore whoever relaxes one of the least of these commandments and teaches others to do the same will be called least in the kingdom of heaven, but whoever does them and teaches them will be called great in the kingdom of heaven. For I tell you, unless your righteousness exceeds that of the scribes and Pharisees, you will never enter the kingdom of heaven.

He reinforced the righteous interpretations as the only and eternal rule of the Kingdom/Recreation. Only the grace-created Decalogue-way sufficed for arranging day-by-day gratitude.

This must yet be said: never in Israel's Old Testament history did the Author/authors riddle the narratives with people self-righteously earning credits in the Pharisee/Sadducee manner. Unbelieving Israelites merely switched over to Canaanite, Assyrian, Babylonian, or Grecian/Roman idolatries, each in marked contrast to the Religion. The Tradition-of-the-Elders people, however, developed a religiosity specifically engineered to caricature the Religion. Because of its aggressive allures, Jesus prodded the Oral Law aside, its misleading imitation incapable of the righteous imperatives specific to the Kingdom/Recreation. He spurned those pretentious 613 manmade rules and denounced their covetous orientation. His Decalogue only structured gratitude.

To make the Decalogue come alive for thankfulness in the new dispensation, the Teacher presented the emergent Church with illustrations of biblical interpretations. In each instance, he started out, saying, "you have heard," thereby referencing the incompetence of the Oral Law, Matthew 5:21–48. At rightly condemning Pharisee/Sadducee teachings, Jesus shone the light of candor on four commandments, which Matthew *chose* possibly because the men of the Oral Law by misusing these holy dictates perpetrated the worst abuses—to *magnify* the Jewish god.

One, expressive of the Sixth Commandment: the Pharisees/Sadducees' hereditary bias concisely stated, Matthew 5:21, "You have heard that it was said by those of old, 'You shall not murder, and whoever murders will be liable to judgment.'"[35] Though superficially correct, the Sadducees assumed this mandate referred to physical killing only; the leaders of Old Israel found themselves fully righteous, faultless in supposedly lesser sorts of murder.

The Christ, the original designer and author of the Decalogue, Exodus 31:18, opened the Sixth Commandment into its wholeness. Matthew 5:22, "But I say to you that ever one who is angry with his brother will be liable to judgment; whoever insults his brother will be liable to the council; and whoever says 'You fool!' will be liable to the hell of fire." By declaring anger a form of murder, the Son of God willed entire gratitude with respect to the Sixth, not superficiality, not caricature, not even shadow performances to cover evil dispositions, but wholehearted thanksgiving. Whereas the Pharisees/Sadducees found self-serving satisfaction in posturing, Jesus spelled out the literal impact of this commandment, unreserved conformity.

Two, expressive of the Seventh Commandment: omniscient Jesus capably read also high-ranking Pharisee/Sadducee thought patterns. Matthew 5:27, "You have heard that it was said, 'You shall not commit adultery.'" Old Israel's leaders judged themselves according to surface interpretations fastened in the Oral Law.[36] The Lord Jesus interpreted the Seventh uprightly. Matthew 5:28, "But I say to you that everyone who looks at a woman with lustful intent has already committed adultery with her in his heart." The Legislator hereby exposed the fornicative hearts of Old Israel's leading classes.[37]

Again, relative to the Seventh Commandment: Matthew 5:31, "It was also said, 'Whoever divorces his wife, let him give her a certificate of divorce.'" As Jesus taught in Matthew 19:3–9; Mark 10:11–12; Luke 16:18, the Jews misread and misapplied Deuteronomy 24:1–4; Romans 7:1–3. Against a leadership devoid of righteousness, Jesus reset for all time the Kingdom/Recreation's marital/sexual intimacies, nothing short of consensual holiness, 1 Corinthians 7:1–5.

Three, expressive of the Ninth Commandment: the Lord and Savior at condemning Pharisee/Sadducee deviancy, simultaneously commanded

---

35. Oral Law #278.

36. Oral Law #102.

37. Romans 2:3 expresses the Pharisaic/Sadduceic decadence then. "Do you suppose, O man—you who judge those who practice such things and yet do them yourself—that you will escape the judgment of God?" Malachi 2:13–16 examples such fraudulence.

heart observance of this mandate. Matthew 5:33, "Again, you have heard that it was said to those of old, 'You shall not swear falsely, but shall perform to the Lord what you have sworn.'" Against that virtue of honesty, Jesus presented ingrained Pharisee/Sadducee deception and deceit, the Corban-tradition,[38] Matthew 15:1–9; Mark 7:1–8, indeed, the entire Tradition of the Elders, Matthew 23:1–36; Mark 12:38–40; Luke 20:45–47. Those masters of deceit caught the unwary in tightly woven nets. In contrast, Jesus revealed the Ninth's entirety of holiness. Matthew 5:34–37, "But I say to you, Do not take an oath at all, either by heaven, for it is the throne of God, or by the earth, for it is his footstool, or by Jerusalem, for it is the city of the great King.[39] And do not take an oath by your head, for you cannot make one hair white or black. Let what you say be simply 'Yes' or 'No'; anything more than this comes from evil." James 5:12. Oral Law specifics conveniently overruled the Ninth's honesty. Hence, the Lord of heaven and earth mandated holiness in contractual language, thrusting trust into the Kingdom/Recreation's communal transactions.

Four, expressive of the neighbor-love commandment: Pharisees/Sadducees advocated the Law of Retribution factually—an eye for an eye and a tooth for a tooth—grossly misinterpreting Exodus 21:23–25 and demanding sweet revenge for every hurt.[40] Jesus in the midst of that hate, revealed the heart of the Decalogue, evidence of the Kingdom/Recreation's eternal holiness. Matthew 5:44–48,

> But I say to you, Love your enemies and pray for those who persecute you, so that you may be sons of your Father who is in heaven. For he makes his sun rise on the evil and on the good, and sends rain on the just and the unjust. For if you love those who love you, what reward do you have? Do not even the tax collectors do the same? And if you greet only your brothers, what more are you doing than others? Do not even the Gentiles do the same? You therefore must be perfect, as your heavenly Father is perfect.

Old Israel's ruling class studiously ignored Leviticus 19:18. "You shall not take vengeance or bear a grudge against the sons of your own people, but you shall love your neighbor as yourself: I am the LORD." To be difficult, those men of means intended revenge for every slight.

---

38. First Timothy 5:8, "... if anyone does not provide for his relatives, and especially for members of his household, he has denied the faith and is worse than an unbeliever."

39. Psalm 48:1–2.

40. Lamech, Genesis 4:23–24, set the pace for revenge.

Instead of such hatefulness, Jesus, full of grace and truth, declared with the majesty of divinity, Matthew 5:39–42, "But I say to you, Do not resist the one who is evil. But if anyone slaps you on the right cheek, turn to him the other also. And if anyone would sue you and take your tunic, let him have your cloak as well. And if anyone forces you to go one mile, go with him two miles. Give to the one who begs from you, and do not refuse the one who would borrow from you." This mercy-laden reconfiguration of the *lex taliones* created community as Jesus willed. Matthew 6:3–4, "But when you give to the needy, do not let your left hand know what your right hand is doing, so that your giving may be in secret. And your Father who sees in secret will reward you." In this manner, he granted hope to the downtrodden, mercy to the lost, and liberty to the oppressed, even repentance for the hateful.

This teaching wiped away all ground for revenge, even any avenging of blood, Numbers 35:12, to leave vengeance to the Lord Jesus, Romans 12:19; Hebrews 10:30.

Throughout these wise reconstitutions in the light of candor, Christ Jesus faced down the darkness, forced native hatred into defeat, and compelled into the open the whole of neighbor love. Luke 10:25–28; Mark 12:28–34; Matthew 22:34–40,

> But when the Pharisees heard that he had silenced the Sadducees, they gathered together. And one of them, a lawyer, asked him a question to test him. "Teacher, which is the great commandment in the Law?" And he said to him, "You shall love the LORD your God with all your heart and with all your soul and with all your mind. This is the great and first commandment. And a second is like it: You shall love your neighbor as yourself. On these two commandments depend all the Law and the Prophets."

As the Lord and Savior loved the New Church with trinitarian passion and she loves him as well as respective neighbors, Romans 13:8–14, the people of the Church, that is, the citizens of the Kingdom/Recreation, grow into the powers of life.

During his determined walking from Galilee through Jerusalem to Golgotha, Jesus reinstituted with finality the holy directives of the Mosaic Law as also the basis for adjudication, non-compliance the evidence of damnation; the whole of the Decalogue encompassed as well as structured gratitude. Therefore throughout Matthew 5:21–48, he clarified its heights and depths, its widths and breadths for gratitude.

Now, in sum, the Lord Jesus convinced and convinces believers to activate the Decalogue first entrusted to Moses and Israel. Unending as the New

Israel,[41] the Church out of gratitude for salvation lives the Ten Commandments—to the exclusion of Human Rights formulations, Mohammedan justice, Hindu inclusivity; etc. People living the crucial decalogual imperatives, inclusive the case studies in Exodus, Leviticus, Numbers, and Deuteronomy, mark out the boundaries of the Kingdom/Recreation.

Judging Criteria

With the Son-of-Man naming, Jesus revealed the cruciality of judging in his kingship; he, the Arbitrator, judges all peoples, first those of the Church, solely by one standard, the Decalogue. Post-Ascension, seated at the right hand[42] of God the Father, Isaiah 6:1; Acts 2:33, 7:55; Ephesians 1:20; etc., he is the supreme court and the bar of justice, supremely cognizant of all heart secrets and public sins. Whatever else the Son-of-Man name may call forth—awe, deference, and reverence—first and foremost it designates Jesus the righteous and holy Judge over heaven and earth, impartially administering the divine judiciary by the proclamation of the word from within the Church.

In the first dispensation, King David enacted judgeship as a decisive catalyst for God-praising government and for grounding his monarchial office. A delinquent judiciary destabilizes and demoralizes rulership. Hence, at authoring Psalm 8:6, he knew himself the then-and-there son of man in creating a righteous rule of justice.

> You have given him dominion over the works of your hands;
> you have put all things under his feet.

Out of that biblically meritorious vision, he rebuilt the judiciary based on the animating Mosaic Law, Exodus 18:24–25; Deuteronomy 1:9–18, and deputized unbribable men to sit in judgment over errant covenant citizens, 1 Chronicles 26:29–32. Once David had called the son-of-man name to life, this designation became definitive for Jesus' judgeship.

---

41. Argyle. *God in the New Testament,* 21, "By the representative and vicarious sacrifice of His suffering and death, and by the victory of his exaltation, He accomplished the divinely appointed redemptive destiny of Israel, and in that destiny the new Israel, the Christian church, is called to share as the Spirit-filled, saved and saving community of Christ."

42. Seating at the right hand of God the Father never meant a place of secondary importance. Rather, in this manner, God the Father recognized and affirmed Jesus in his humanity and divinity as the authoritative Judge, which belief the Holy Spirit creates in all Christianized hearts.

Later, in time nearer the Incarnation, the LORD God, that is, the Messiah, defined Ezekiel's prophetic ministry in terms of the son-of-man naming. Repeatedly, Yahweh addressed him as the son of man, the prophetic judge justifying Israel's Exile.

Hence, prestigiously, from out of the Old Testament ages, the Christ stabilized normative judgment by the son-of-man assignment.

The Son of Man recreated and outright owned the holy office of judging, Matthew 8:20; Luke 9:58; John 9:35–37, 12:48–50. At the healing of the paralytic and in the hearing of Pharisaic faultfinders, Jesus explicitly acknowledged his juridical identity, Matthew 9:6; Mark 2:10; Luke 5:24, ". . . that you may know that the Son of Man has authority on earth to forgive sins—he said to the man who was paralyzed—'I say to you, rise, pick up your bed and go home.'" Afterward, throughout the Synoptics, Jesus knew himself the Judge.[43] Poignantly, he authored the Parable of the Great Judgment, its apocalyptic language compelling. Matthew 25:31–32, "When the Son of Man comes in his glory and all the angels with him, then he will sit on his glorious throne. Before him will be gathered all the nations, and he will separate people one from another as a shepherd separates the sheep from the goats." By this decisive parable, the Son of Man illumed the first and great Judgment,[44] the Crucifixion, that with the Resurrection and the Ascension set the last days into motion. Unflinchingly, Jesus in day-to-day ministry declared himself the Son of Man, the reigning arbiter of the decalogual standard. Simultaneously, he spurned all other legal standards, certainly the Oral and the Roman Laws.

Jesus explicitly affirmed his judging office. John 5:22, "The Father judges no one, but has given all judgment to the Son." Again, pertinent to his humanity, John 5:27, "And [the Father] has given him authority to execute judgment, because he the Son of Man." God the Father's confirmation of Jesus' rulership over the high court of justice acknowledged him the Arbiter over all legal arbiters, John 8:16. This Jesus asserted once more; John 9:39, "For judgment I came into this world, that those who do not see may see, and those who see may become blind." In the nastiest ferments of Jewish unwillingness to concede defeat, cast the Oral Law aside, and recognize the Son of Man the

---

43. Matthew 10:23; Luke 7:34. Matthew 12:8; Luke 6:5. Matthew 13:41. Matthew 16:27–28; Luke 9:26. Matthew 17:9; Mark 9:9. Matthew 17:12. Matthew 17:22; Mark 9:31; Luke 9:22. Matthew 20:18; Mark 10:33; Luke 8:31. Matthew 24:29–31; Mark 13:24–27; Luke 21:25–28. Matthew 24:37, 39. Matthew 26:24; Mark 14:21; Luke 22:22. Matthew 26:2, 24, 45; Mark 14:41. Etc.

44. Forecasting Satan's fateful falling from heaven indicates a little of the Judgment's radicality, John 12:31; Luke 10:18.

Judge rather than the Sanhedrin, they attempted to lure Christians back into an area synagogue, the very legitimacy of which now at stake.

On the morning of Crucifixion Day, the Lord and Savior provoked the conceited and venomous Sanhedrin that measured him by the malfunctioning Oral Law to accomplish what the Trinity had foreordained in eternity, the condemnation of the Son of Man according to the Oral Law. In that dark vortex of calamitous misjudging, Jesus, omnipotent through his divinity, *unseated* his incompetent judges. Matthew 26:64; Mark 14:62; Luke 22:69, "... from now on the Son of Man shall be seated at the right of the power of God." From the seat of ultimate authority that the Trinity in the forever and ever had assigned him, the Son of Man solemnly informed the Sanhedrin, and thereby all Pharisees/Sadducees, that he alone owned the almighty judgeship, while they sank under biases and judgmental verdicts.[45]

The trial then invoked apocalyptic visions, the world and the universe caught up in the turbulences of the last days. Luke 17:22–37, 21:25–28, 34–38; Matthew 24:36–37; Mark 13:32–37. With the trial and the Crucifixion, the Lord Jesus began the quickening of the second and final judgment, hammering home multiple woes of condemnation, Luke 20:45–47; Matthew 23:1–36. At hastening the Parousia, the Lord Jesus exposed the mystery of lawlessness,[46] 2 Thessalonians 2:7, which offered most appealing off-ramps from the high road into swamplands of damnation.

Jesus also installed the Twelve, minus Judas Iscariot and plus Matthias, to represent him in the ecclesial judging office, to enact justice in his name. Luke 22:28–29, "You are those who have stayed with me in my trials, and I assign to you, as my Father assigned to me, a kingdom, that you may eat and drink at my table in my kingdom and sit on thrones judging the twelve tribes of Israel." Revelation 4:4. The Apostles condemned the Old Church's Oral Law and called the New Church to her one foundation, Christ Jesus, 1 Corinthians 3:11.

Now mocking or ignoring the Arbiter and his judiciary bodes ill for all ingrates, foremost those still hypocritically concealed within congregational membership, 1 Peter 4:17.

---

45. With Nicodemus a lone exception, John 19:39.

46. Farrow, Douglas, "Confessing Christ Coming." 133–48, in Seitz. *Nicene Christianity*, 145, "The mystery of iniquity is at work in the church and at work in this particular way: its theologians and its preachers no longer trouble themselves much to confess Christ coming. The Scripture is read, the creed is said, the liturgy prayed; the word of his coming is there and cannot be avoided, yet it is widely ignored by those who speak to and for the church, who seem always to have something more pressing to say. Ignored too is the warning about great apostasy, a defection to Antichrist."

Was not that the appeal of the self-righteousness dominating Pharisaism and Sadduceism?

Elective Criteria

Against the Jews and Romans who imagined competences at earning idolatrous salvations, Jesus revealed the originality and eternality of the Atonement. John 6:44–45; Luke 10:21–22; Matthew 11:25–27,

> . . . Jesus declared, "I thank you, Father, Lord of heaven and earth, that you have hidden these things from the wise and understanding and revealed them to little children; yes, Father, for such was your gracious will. All things have been handed over to me by my Father, and no one knows the Son except the Father, and no one knows the Father except the Son and anyone to whom the Son chooses to reveal him."

This immovable and unalterable source of redemption, eternally prior to the creation of the universe,[47] abides for all eternity, John 6:39, 10:28–29, 17:2–3, 6. Jesus actualized this predestinarian teaching in and with the Crucifixion; he died to atone for the guilt of sinning, that is, for all whom God the Father assigned to receive the grace of redemption. Jesus' atoning work on the Cross brought alive the actuality of the Expiation.

Conversely, Pharisee/Sadducee and Roman classes of salvation rested in quagmires of religiosities. The perishable gods and goddesses of these perversions of the Religion craved enslaved followers in which these life-suffocating deities stirred up addictive behaviors—for the Jews at that time submission to the Tradition of the Elders and for the Romans capitulation to Caesarism as well as multiple elevated figures pulled out on feast days. In the marketplaces of idolatrous energy, these little gods gained firmer hold on true believers and made them watch meager down payments on salvation burn away in disappointment. Immoderate as well as unsatisfiable demands of pseudo-deities condemned communities of worshipers to live in doubt, never assured of sufficient *funds* to satisfy impossible moral meters.

Jesus, in whose hands life and death, throughout the ages called and calls the elect to appear before him. Therefore, upon the Exodus, Israel, the sole elect nation, Deuteronomy 7:6–11,[48] stood in worship at the base of the Sinai. Therefore, now the elect come out of the disingenuous anomalies of religiosity to bear the lively burden of grace. Matthew 11:28–30,

---

47. Rhodes. *Christ Before the Manger,* 14, ". . . prior to the beginning of time, God conceived a grand and glorious plan for humankind (Eph. 1:11). The plan was conceived *in eternity,* but would be carried out by God *in time.* That which was eternally determined *before the ages* would be brought to fruition *in the ages.*"

48. The Lord Jesus majestically accomplishes Israel's election—not all Israel is Israel—as recorded in Romans 9:1—11:26.

> Come to me, all who labor and are heavy laden, and I will give you rest. Take my yoke upon you, and learn from me, for I am gentle and lowly in heart, and you will find rest for your souls. For my yoke is easy, and my burden is light.

Therefore now, gracious to the extreme, the Son of Man, judging by actually prehistoric trinitarian decisions, calls all chosen to know the salvation cemented in eternity and concretized on the Cross. Romans 8:29–30 lays open the eternality of predestination and projects the light of the Cross, fastened in time/space, to impute irreversibly the powers of redemption. Everyone whom the Father foreknew he predestined to conform to the image of his Son,[49] and those he predestined he also called, and those whom he called he also justified, and those whom he justified in the Crucifixion he also glorified, or sanctified. The eternality of the Atonement rests in the eternal wellspring of grace overflowing with Jesus' assurances of the divine Yes.

Apostle Paul in Ephesians 1:3–10, the heart of which 3–6, opens the grace of predestination, summing up election in its fullness.

> Blessed be the God and Father of our Lord Jesus Christ, who has blessed us in Christ with every spiritual blessing in the heavenly places, even as he chose us in him before the foundation of the world, that we should be holy and blameless before him. In love he predestined us for adoption as sons through Jesus Christ, according to the purpose of his will, to the praise of his glorious grace, with which he has blessed us in the Beloved.

Apostles Peter and Paul moved and motivate believers to ensure the calling to election, Acts 13:48; 2 Timothy 1:9; Titus 1:2, 1 Peter 1:2; 2 Peter 1:10, by gratefully living the Kingdom/Recreation's Decalogue.

The rise of Semi-Pelagianism and its near relative, Arminianism, meant to confuse the biblical predestinarian teaching. Now numerous normally sane human beings hanging in reprobation above the pit of damnation find they must choose for or against salvation; the unwilling may even refuse the Yes of Christ Jesus. Out of mismanaged freedom of religion or freedom of the will, they insist with boss-energy to possess the will to believe or deny the Gospel in a way that overrides the word of the omnipotent Trinity. Poor people, misguided by the misguided, determine that they own the first and the final authority over the Trinity—disparaging God the Father's choosing,

---

49. Of enduring import: the Son *lives and works* at the very center of Romans 8:29–30; without him nothing of election comes true.

God the Son's calling, and God the Spirit's vitality—thereby in orgies of revivalism[50] repetitiously demanding the evidence of the Faith in question.

To discourage the vanity of human choosing, Apostle John also at the Christ's behest called the elect into the glory of the Light:

> John 3:27, "A person cannot receive even one thing unless it is given him from heaven."
>
> John 6:37, "All that the Father gives me will come to me, and whoever comes to me I will never cast out."
>
> John 6:44a, "No one can come to me unless the Father who sent me draws him."
>
> John 6:65, "... no one can come to me unless it is granted him by the Father."[51]

Believers never twist the Scriptures about in Arminian ways to magnify themselves, for predestination both in election and in reprobation glorifies only the ineffable Trinity, Ephesians 3:11. Paul recorded the eternal affirmative of election, Romans 8:31–39, and confirmed the factual that no power in heaven and under heaven can separate the elect from his omnipotence.

Shepherding Criteria

Ministering in holiness, itinerant Jesus traversed Canaan-land to herd his scattered sheep into one flock. This shepherd-analogy recalls Psalms 23:1–3, 80:1a, as well as Isaiah 40:11, 53:7–8, Ezekiel 34:11–16, and Micah 5:6. Such pastoral passion exposes and convicts sheep-stealers and sheep-abusers, Jeremiah 23:1–4; Ezekiel 34:1–10, shepherds eating the flock. Ezekiel 34:23, 36:38; Matthew 9:35–38,

> ... Jesus went throughout all the cities and villages, teaching in their synagogues and proclaiming the gospel of the kingdom and healing every disease and every affliction. When he saw the crowds, he had compassion on them, because they were harassed and helpless, like sheep without a shepherd. Then he said

---

50. McDonald. *The Armageddon Factor*, 124–25, "... worshippers suddenly found themselves convulsed in spasms of uncontrollable laughter, thrashing on the floor, a few even barking like dogs. The phenomenon continued for more than two months, making headlines around the world and attracting as many as a thousand people a night, some flying from Africa and Asia in a desperate bid to catch the miracle of holy laughter that became known as the Toronto Blessing."

51. This revelation continues: John 10:29, 13:18, 15:16, 17:2, 6, 9, 12; etc.

to his disciples, "The harvest is plentiful, but the laborers are few; therefore pray earnestly to the Lord of the harvest to send out laborers into his harvest."

As the Shepherd, the Lord and Savior sent out under-shepherds, the Twelve, for missionarying in synagogues, marketplaces, and Israelite towns to initiate ingathering of the flock, the body of believers unified in praising, indeed, in magnifying the Trinity, Matthew 10:5–15; Mark 6:7–13; Luke 9:1–6. Untiringly, Jesus manifested the holy intensity of the Shepherd illustrated by unforgettable stories, one of which the Parable of the Lost Sheep, Matthew 18:10–14; Luke 15:3–7. Constant awareness of the Matthew 25:31–46 sheep-goat distinction and the believers' names in the Revelation 13:8 book of life sparkles in living the Christian commitment.

With the shepherd-parables of John 10:1–18, Jesus asserted 1) that he is the sole way into salvation as pictured in Isaiah 53:7, 2) that he is the spotless Lamb of God, John 1:29, 36, and 3) that he is the Good Shepherd, the great Shepherd, Hebrews 13:20, and the Chief Shepherd, 1 Peter 5:4, missing none, not even the least lamb. All other purported possible ways of salvation simulate fentanyl-like induced slumbers, sleepwalking into the abyss.

Prophetic Criteria

Prophetically, throughout the Matthew-Mark-Luke-John Gospel, Jesus in the forthtelling of Israel's history foretold in his ministry the inspirational fervency of the Kingdom/Recreation, the Church its visible presence. He based this projection on the Crucifixion-Resurrection-Ascension glories. By virtue of his divinity and by versatility of his vocal chords, he adjusted the world to embody multiple congregations. His first hearers, all Israelites, listened to the Man and heard him, the Son of God, laying open before their eyes the successive tomorrows of his sovereign rule.

To ready for the Prophet's ministry, John the Baptizer served as the last Old Testament herald, which Matthew, 11:10, and Mark, 1:2, recalled.

After Jesus' baptism, the Baptizer, mission accomplished, became less and less, not with an early retirement payout but radically, by a beheading. The Lord and Savior did not prevent this murder, Matthew 14:1–12; Mark 6:14–29; Luke 9:7–9, lest he and his followers compete with the Prophet and draw Israel away, John 3:30. Rather, in response, Jesus built on precursors' prophetic works, John's too, to recreate the Kingdom/Recreation.

Jesus' foretelling in the forthtelling of Israel's history occupied the Church's interest. He shone first a great light into Galilee, Matthew 4:15–16/ Isaiah 9:1–2. John 4:43–45; Luke 4:14; Mark 1:14–15, "Now after [John the

Baptizer] was arrested, Jesus came into Galilee, proclaiming the gospel of God, and saying, 'The times is fulfilled, and the kingdom of God is at hand; repent and believe in the gospel.'" Contingent on believing the Gospel, Jesus foretold dire persecutory urgencies, Matthew 10:16–23; Mark 13:9–13; Luke 21:10–19. In this register of references, Jesus involved the Twelve directly, revealing the terminal hatred fuming in reprobate hearts, Matthew 10:21–23; Luke 12:2–7; John 15:18. With knowing insight to Pharisee/Sadducee reactions to the Gospel, the Prophet prepared his disciples for the hardships consequent to faithfulness. Matthew 10:32–33,

> So everyone who acknowledges me before men, I will also acknowledge before my Father who is in heaven, but whoever denies me before men, I also will deny before my Father who is in heaven.

Spirit-moved Matthew expanded further upon this toxic animosity in the making. Micah 7:5–6/Matthew 10:34–39, "Do not think that I have come to bring peace to the earth. I have not come to bring peace, but a sword. For I have come to set a man against his father, and a daughter against her mother, and a daughter-in-law against her mother-in-law. And a person's enemies will be those of his own household. Whoever loves father or mother more than me is not worthy of me, and whoever loves son or daughter more than me is not worthy of me. And whoever does not take his cross and follow me is not worthy of me. Whoever finds his life will lose it, and whoever loses his life for my sake will find it." With prophetic intensity, he held up the sword that divides even familial intimacies. So, in various ways, Jesus opened Israel to its continuing Gospel-denying mean-mindedness.

Contrariwise, the Son of God promised cumulative blessings. Matthew 10:40–42, to the Twelve, "Whoever receives you receives me, and whoever receives me receives him who sent me. The one who receives a prophet because he is a prophet will receive a prophet's reward, and the one who receives a righteous person because he is a righteous person will receive a righteous person's reward. And whoever gives one of these little ones even a cup of cold water because he is a disciple, truly, I say you, he will by no means lose his reward." Now starting with these men and looking (far) ahead, Jesus ingrained in each, except Judas Iscariot, the blessed values of apostolic trustworthiness.

Responsive to disruptive scribes and Pharisees who out of an idolatrous mindset called for a miracle, Jesus recalled two thought-provoking people from the past. Luke 11:29–32; Matthew 12:38–45, "An evil and adulterous generation seeks for a sign, but no sign will be given to it except the sign of the prophet Jonah. For just as Jonah was three days and three nights in the belly of the great fish, so will the Son of Man be three days and three nights in the heart of the earth. The men of Nineveh will rise up at the judgment with this generation and condemn it, for they repented at the preaching of Jonah, and behold, something greater than Jonah is here. The queen of the South will rise up at the judgment with this generation and condemn it, for she came from the ends of the earth to hear the wisdom of Solomon, and behold, something greater than Solomon is here." Jesus refused every temptation to degrade himself into a magician entertaining hostiles.

Accurately insightful, Jesus foreknew the Crucifixion-Resurrection actuality for his humanity relative to the substitutionary atonement, which he thrice foretold to the Twelve: Matthew 16:21-23; Mark 8:31—9:1; Luke 9:22-27. Matthew 17:22-23; Mark 9:30-32; Luke 9:43-45. Matthew 20:17-19; Mark 10:21-22; Luke 18:31-34/24:6-7. Such was the function of the Parable of the Tenants, Luke 20:9-18; Mark 12:1-12; Matthew 21:33-46; by the telling, he opened with detail his immediate future in the Crucifixion. Even as the Synoptists, John pressed home Jesus' structuring of tomorrow, 2:19, 8:28, 12:33, 13:36, prophetically stipulating the Resurrection, 11:25. Nothing was hidden from his omniscience and unwavering he walked to the Cross. With the intensity of conviction, he knew the agony appointed for his humanity, and its import.

Omnisciently, the Lord and Savior laid out before his disciples/apostles the Trinity's basic tenets for the hope of the Eschaton, the foundation of which the Crucifixion-Resurrection-Ascension history. Matthew 22:29-33; Mark 12:28-34, "And one of the scribes came up and heard [the Sadducees] disputing with [Jesus], and seeing that [Jesus] answered them well, asked him, 'Which commandment is the most important of all?' Jesus answered, 'The most important is, "Hear, O Israel: the Lord our God, the Lord is one. And you shall love the Lord your God with all your heart and with all your soul and with all your mind and with all your strength." The second is this: "You shall love your neighbor as yourself." There is no other commandment greater than these.' And the scribe said to him, 'You are right, Teacher. You have truly said that he is one, and there is no other besides him. And to love [Jesus] with all the heart and with all the understanding and with all the strength, and to love one's neighbor as oneself, is much more than all whole burnt offerings and sacrifices.' And when Jesus saw that he answered wisely, he said to him, 'You are not far from the kingdom of God.' And after that no one dared to ask him any more questions." For he, its Author, knew the Law better than all accumulated scribes and Pharisees.

According to Apostle John, this love of neighbor occurs solely while glorifying the Son of Man and, simultaneously, God the Father, 13:31-35, 15:12-15; such loving informs all of the activity of God the Holy Spirit.

At the same time, unapologetically, Jesus verbally shot seven woes into this Pharisaism, Matthew 23:1–12, 25:31–46; Mark 12:38–40; Luke 20:45–47; these afflictions began immediately, two of which, Matthew 23:13–15, "But woe to you, scribes and Pharisees, hypocrites! For you shut the kingdom of heaven in people's faces. For you neither enter yourselves nor allow those who would enter to go in. Woe to you, scribes and Pharisees, hypocrites! For you travel across sea and land to make a single proselyte, and when he becomes a proselyte, you make him twice as much a child of hell as yourselves." Jesus made them walk *open-eyed* into damnation. For eradicating the Tradition of the Elders, Jesus announced the ruin of Jerusalem and the Temple, both thoroughly vilified by the sins of the Oral Law. Luke 21:20–24; Mark 13:14–23; Matthew 24:15–28. The Lord and Savior willed a new temple, the Church, 1 Corinthians 3:16–17.

More eschatologically penetrative, knowing the way to the Day of Judgment and structuring the plans thereof, Jesus with omniscient perception and human vocalization spoke of fake messiahs polluting the Crucifixion-Resurrection-Ascension history, post-Pentecost. Luke 21:5–38; Mark 13:1–37; Matthew 24:1–51, of which 4–8,

> See that no one leads you astray. For many will come in my name, saying, "I am the Christ," and they will lead many astray. And you will hear of wars and rumors of wars. See that you are not alarmed, for this must take place, but the end is not yet. For nation will rise against nation, and kingdom against kingdom, and there will be famines and earthquakes in various places. All these are but the beginning of the birth pains.

Thus, in clearly articulated Aramaic, Jesus out of his divine omniscience thoroughly organized and equipped the New Church through the ministry of the Apostles for the lively way to and into the Eschaton.

With respect to his humanity, Jesus acknowledged limits. When (the mother of) the sons of Zebedee, James and John, sought preferential treatment, Jesus declared that ranking in the celestial throne area belonged to God the Father, Matthew 20:20–28; Mark 10:35–45. Similarly, to halt a competitive spirit among the Twelve, Luke 22:24–27, he willed the peace of the Kingdom/Recreation, Mark 10:45; Matthew 20:28, the whole of which God the Father had planned, even as the day of the Eschaton, Matthew 24:36; Mark 13:32. At times, Jesus 1) manifested the glories of his divinity; and at other times 2) acknowledged his human limitations.

At the foretelling within the forthtelling, the Son of God's humanity and divinity interactively cooperated without the one becoming the other.

Anti-coveting Criteria

With Aramaic fluency and by divine omniscience—the two fully synchronized without violating either the divine or the human—Jesus built up the wisdom teaching he originated in the Old Testament. This wisdom literature—Job, Psalms, Proverbs, Ecclesiastes, and the Song of Songs—exposed and exposes the root of all evil, covetousness. Such then brings Matthew 5:1—7:27 and Luke 6:20—49 into the open. These sayings along with parables and similar teachings penetrate squalid depths of covetousness, to scrutinize as well as outright eradicate any such slavish submission to the hereditary foe, the Serpent. Jesus' expressive wisdom discards Pharisaic and Sadduceic works-righteousness, the duplicitous merit-economy of that theocratic idolatry.

Throughout this wisdom teaching,[52] Jesus covered key areas of faith and life expressive of the presence of the Kingdom. Matthew 4:17, "From that time Jesus began to preach, saying, 'Repent for the kingdom of heaven is at hand.'" To cleanse the Church for the first and great judgment, the Crucifixion, he walked about Galilee, teaching in synagogues and in open places, wherever he chose to command a hearing.

1

Listeners respected the authority with which the Lord and Savior spoke; in fact, at first they were astonished at his prudential instruction, Mark 1:27; Matthew 7:28–29. Paradoxically, on his walking round-abouts from Galilee to Jerusalem and Jerusalem to Galilee, many listened and many towered higher in murderous hatred, seeking to kill him. To Pharisaic hearted, Matthew 11:1, 12:33–37,

> Either make the tree good and its fruit good, or make the tree bad and its fruit bad, for the tree is known by its fruit. You brood of vipers! How can you speak good, when you are evil? For out of the abundance of the heart the mouth speaks. The good person out of his good treasure brings forth good, and the evil person out of his evil treasure brings forth evil. I tell you, on the day of judgment people will give account of every careless word

---

52. Toon and Spiceland. *One God in Trinity*, 12–13, "He says that his words will last for ever (Mark 13:31) and his presence and teaching bring responsibility to his generation; his generation is unfavourably compared with that in Sodom and Gomorrah (Matt. 10:15; 11:20–24). Indeed, men will be judged by his words (John 12:40–50) and his authority to forgive sins is provocatively related in Mark 2:1–10 with his power to heal."

they speak, for by your words you will be justified, and by your words you will be condemned.

In this teaching ministry, the Lord thoroughly excoriated Israel's cauldron of enmity and therewith its works-righteousness, thus calling the Old Church to acknowledge the radicality of the coming judgment.

This judgment, the first and the great, controlled the core issues of life, Mark 7:14–23; Matthew 15:10–20. "And he called the people to him and said to them, 'Hear and understand: it is not what goes into the mouth that defiles a person, but what comes out of the mouth; this defiles a person.' Then the disciples came and said to him, 'Do you know that the Pharisees were offended when they heard this saying?' He answered, 'Every plant that my heavenly Father has not planted will be rooted up. Let them alone; they are blind guides. And if the blind lead the blind, both will fall into a pit.' But Peter said to him, 'Explain the parable to us.' And he said, 'Are you still without understanding? Do you not see that whatever goes into the mouth passes into the stomach and is expelled? But what comes out of the mouth proceeds from the heart, and this defiles a person. For out of the heart come evil thoughts, murder, adultery, sexual immorality, theft, false witness, slander. These are what defile a person." Jesus listed these sinful maneuverings as products of covetousness. "But to eat with unwashed hands does not defile anyone.'" Self-righteous Pharisaic poison had infiltrated pestilential heart-depths, counteracting the infallibly cleansing word. Matthew 16:5–12; Mark 8:18–21; Luke 9:23–26, "And he said to all, 'If anyone would come after me, let him deny himself and take up his cross daily and follow me. For whoever would save his life will lose it, but whoever loses his life for my sake will save it. For what does it profit a man if he gains the whole world and loses or forfeits himself? For whoever is ashamed of me and of my words, of him will the Son of Man be ashamed when he comes in his glory and the glory of the Father and of the holy angels.'" This pastoral ethos, typical of Jesus' wisdom teaching, restricted and choked off the mercurial Pharisaic merit-economy.

With these and more wisdom teachings, Jesus cursed covetousness that his chosen joyfully live the Faith, even in unfavorable conditions.

2

Jesus exposed original sinning by parables. Luke 8:10; Isaiah 6:9/Mark 4:11–12; Isaiah 6:9–10/Matthew 13:10–17,

> ... the disciples came and said to [Jesus], "Why do you speak to them in parables?" And he answered them, "To you it has been

given to know the secrets of the kingdom of heaven, but to them it has not been given. For to the one who has, more will be given, and he will have an abundance, but from the one who has not, even what he has will be taken away. This is why I speak to them in parables, because seeing they do not see, and hearing they do not hear, nor do they understand. Indeed, in their case the prophecy of Isaiah is fulfilled that says:

> "You will indeed hear but not understand,
> and you will indeed see but never perceive.
> For this people's heart has grown dull,
> and with their ears they can barely hear,
> and their eyes they have closed,
> lest they should see with their eyes and hear with their ears
> and understand with their heart and turn,
> and I would heal them."

But blessed are your eyes, for they see, and your ears, for they hear. For truly, I say to you, many prophets and righteous people longed to see what you see, and did not see it, and to hear what you hear, and did not hear it."

In this course of teaching, the Teacher polarized Israel; he separated the still comparatively few who believed the Gospel from all who found they controlled the fount of living.

With this singular purpose, Jesus directed the Parable of the Sower to the disciples and to large crowds. Matthew 13:1-9; Luke 8:4-8; Mark 4:3-9,

> Listen! A sower went out to sow. And as he sowed, some seed fell along the path, and the birds came and devoured it. Other seed fell on rocky ground, where it did not have much soil, and immediately it sprang up, since it had no depth of soil. And when the sun rose, it was scorched, and since it had no root, it withered away. Other seed fell among thorns, and the thorns grew up and choked it, and it yielded no grain. And other seed fell into good soil and produced grain, growing up and increasing and yielding thirtyfold and sixtyfold and a hundredfold.

With similar attentiveness, to expose and counter covetousness, Jesus taught the Parable of the Weeds, Matthew 13:24-30; Mark 4:26-29; the Parable of the Mustard Seed, Matthew 13:31-32; Mark 4:30-32; Luke 13:18-19; the Parable of the Leaven, Matthew 13:33; Luke 13:20-21; the Parable of the Hidden Treasure, Matthew 13:44; the Parable of the Pearl of Great Value, Matthew 13:45-46; the Parable of the Net, Matthew 13:47-50; the Parable of the Householder, Matthew 20:1-16; the Parable of the Two Sons, Matthew 21:28-32; the Parable of the Wicked Tenants, Matthew 21:33-46; Mark 12:1-12; Luke 20:9-18; the Parable of the Rich Man and Lazarus, Luke 16:19-31; the Parable of the Persistent Widow, Luke 18:1-8; the Parable of the Pharisee and the Tax Collector, Luke 18:9-14; and the Parable of the Ten Minas, Luke 19:11-27. Each of these stories with positive momentum comes to the same point, the ruination of covetousness.

Jesus moved onto the Parable of the Marriage Feast, Matthew 22:1-14, or the Parable of the Great Banquet, Luke 14:15-24, always with the same elemental cut and thrust. Matthew 13:34-35. "All these [keys to wisdom] Jesus said to the crowds in parables; indeed, he said nothing to them without a parable. This was to fulfil what was spoken by the prophet,

> I will open my mouth in parables;
> I will utter what has been hidden since the foundation of the
> world.
> Psalm 78:2

3

The Serpent shrewdly aroused covetous hungers, social and material. Through such compelling appetites for either sort of prosperity, he agitated slow fires and wild flames of original sinning to entice individual and synagogual cravings in Israelites, and beyond in Parthians, Medes, Elamites, Mesopotamians, as well as residents from Cappadocia, Pontus, Asia, Phrygia, Pamphylia, Egypt, Libya, Rome, Crete, and Arabia, Jews and proselytes. He condemned every raw and cultured craving seeking satisfaction in social and material wealth evocative of Pharisee/Sadducee religiosity.

Respecting social prominence: Jesus denounced this status-security as a foundation for life, Matthew 18:1-4; Mark 9:33-34; Luke 9:46-48. This Old-Church temperament erupted among the Twelve, for which the Lord took them to task.

As projected in Matthew 18:1-9; Luke 9:46-48; Mark 9:33-37, the Teacher with intensifying energy damned covetousness. In order that humility replace pride, he asked [the Twelve], "What were you discussing on the way? But they kept silent, for on the way they had argued with one another about who was the greatest. And he sat down and called the twelve. And he said to them, 'If anyone would be first, he must be last of all and servant of all.' And he took a child and put him in the midst of them, and taking him in his arms, he said to them, 'Whoever receives one such child in my name receives me, and whoever receives me, receives not me but him who sent me.'" Uncompromisingly, the Lord and Savior directed the Faith at himself and God the Father who had laid the foundation of righteousness, expunging core greediness.

Once more, he condemned this deadening quest for social standing, Matthew 20:20–28; Mark 10:35–45; Luke 22:24–30, in which the wife and the sons of Zebedee, James and John, found stiff rebuke.

The Parable of the Wedding Feast, Luke 14:7–11, preserves the parabolic convention.

> Now [Jesus] told a parable to those who were invited, when he noticed how they chose the places of honor, saying to them, "When you are invited by someone to a wedding feast, do not sit down in a place of honor, lest someone more distinguished than you be invited by him, and he who invited you both will come and say to you, 'Give your place to this person,' and then you will begin with shame to take the lowest place. But when you are invited, go and sit in the lowest place, so that when your host comes he may say to you, 'Friend, move up higher.' Then you will be honored in the presence of all who sit at table with you. For everyone who exalts himself will be humbled, and he who humbles himself will be exalted."

Thus, the Parable of the Wedding Feast[53] further downgrades status-seekers and lovers of pomp in the Kingdom. Yet, in the weak and the arrogant, Satan distorts values of social esteem.

Respecting material prosperity: with sliest pretensions, the Devil sought to divert Jesus off the crucifixion-road; with allures of owning all the kingdoms of the earth minus every twinge of pain, the Evil One fought for his very existence, Matthew 4:8–9; Mark 1:12–13, Luke 4:5–6. Jesus in the hour of temptation outright rejected the Devil's offer.

The omniscient Lord and Savior, creator and owner of the universe, taught that the Devil's flimsy and divisive assumptions regarding wealth opened unfathomable depths of poverty covered over only with out-of-date pretenses. Luke 9:25; Mark 8:36; Matthew 16:26, "For what will it profit a man if he gains the whole world and forfeits his soul?"[54] This sorry descent into ultimate pennilessness Jesus merged into the wealth of wisdom, Matthew 6:24p, "You cannot serve God and money." Mammonized life-foundations

---

53. Proverbs 25:6–7, "Do not put yourself forward in the king's presence or stand in the place of the great, for it is better to be told, 'Come up here,' than to be put lower in the presence of a noble."

54. Isaiah 51:8; Ecclesiastes 5:10, "He who loves money will not be satisfied with money, nor he who loves wealth with his income; this also is vanity."

starve hearts of basic nutrients. Eternal malnutrition, the Gentiles' living lot, makes even death worthless.

Jesus commanded the Twelve to live in total reliance on divine providence[55] and teach others the same. Luke 12:22-31; Matthew 6:25:34, specifically 31-34,

> ... do not be anxious, saying, "What shall we eat?" or "What shall we drink?" or "What shall we wear?" For the Gentiles seek after all these things, and your heavenly Father knows that you need them all. But seek first the kingdom of God and his righteousness, and all these things will be added to you.

Independent living sets off a chain of disastrous consequences that at the very least only magnifies misbegotten confidence in wealth. The Corban tradition of Matthew 15:1-9; Mark 7:1-8 exemplified abysmal greediness that removed even care for aging parents burdened by poverty. "If a man tells his father or his mother, 'Whatever you would have gained from me is Corban' (that is, given to God)—then you no longer permit him to do anything for his father or mother, thus making void the word of God by your tradition that you have handed down."[56] With undying denunciation, Jesus denounced the Corban code's moral corruption that depersonalized Jewish religiosity.

The Lord Jesus also doomed a man who, forgiven a spectacular liability, demanded immediate payment of a unimpressive debt, Matthew 18:23-35. This parable uncovers the lengths to which covetousness will drive mammon-worshipers, worship that impairs hearing the Gospel.

The Savior at one point refused embroilment in a rich young ruler's inheritance, Matthew 19:16-30; Mark 10:17-31; Luke 19:18-30. He had through Moses legislated the disposal of legacies, Numbers 27:8; Deuteronomy 21:17, which overruled devilish connivances at stealing. The Law of the First-born, primogeniture, controlled inheritances, Luke 15:31. To sharpen this point of wisdom, the Teacher added Luke 18:24-25; Mark 10:23; Matthew 19:23-23; to his disciples he declared, "Truly, I say to you, only with difficulty will a rich person enter the kingdom of heaven. Again I tell you, it is easier for a camel to go through the eye of a needle[57] than for a rich person to enter the kingdom of God." In this unforgettable manner, the Lord and Savior condemned unsatisfiable hungers for material affluence.

---

55. The Parables of the Hidden Treasure and of the Pearl of Great Value, Matthew 13:44-46, symbolized the significance of the Kingdom, not ultimate scoring in wealth.

56. First Timothy 5:8, "... if anyone does not provide for his relatives, and especially for members of his household, he has denied his faith and is worse than an unbeliever."

57. This "needle" names an easily defensible man-door next to a larger gate.

Matthew 16:24; Luke 14:27; Mark 8:34, "If anyone would come after me, let him deny himself and take up his cross and follow me." Heart-compelled discipleship deadens all spirits of greed, lest Satan, given a handhold, takes all, as the Parable of the Rich Fool clarifies, Luke 12:13–21.

Jesus pictured all-embracing lures of wealth in these transformative stories, the Parable of the Rich Man and Lazarus, Luke 16:19–31, and the Parable of the Tenants, Matthew 21:33–42; Mark 12:1–12; Luke 21:9–19; in the latter, by murdering the servants and the son of the vineyard's owner, the tenants sought possession of the land. Matthew 23:1–3; Mark 12:38–40; Luke 20:45–47, "And in the hearing of all the people [Jesus] said to his disciples, 'Beware of the scribes who like to walk around in long robes, and love greetings in the market places and the best seats in the synagogue and the places of honor at feasts, who devour widows' houses and for a pretense make long prayers. They will receive the greater condemnation.'" In this manner, Jesus opened the dark future for Old-Church leaders, plus all who sheepishly indulged in passions for material gain.

A most condemnable episode of greed? The thirty pieces of silver for which Judas Iscariot *sold* the Lord and Savior into the murderous hands of the Pharisees/Sadducees/Herodians, a betrayal sealed in the dark of night with a fraternal kiss, Matthew 26:14–16, 27:3–10; Mark 14:10–11, 43–50; Luke 22:3–6, 47–53; John 12:2–11, 13:11, 13:21–30.

The Scriptures abuse covetousness, social and/or material, which traps members of the Church in vagaries of cupidity; once so caught, the Teacher guarantees an ending in extreme poverty—isolation in friendlessness and stagnation in scarcity.

4

In his teaching ministry, Jesus revealed *the* exclusive on marriage, sexual intimacy, and family; by wisdom instruction, he condemned every lure destructive of human sexuality, explicitly so. However tempting the covetousness of lapsing into fornicative pleasures, the Lord and Savior, building on the abominations listed in Leviticus 18:1–30, damned any descent into sexual immorality.

First, he severely censured adultery. Matthew 5:27, "You have heard that it was said, 'You shall not commit adultery.'[58] But I say to you that everyone who looks at a woman with lustful intent has already committed adultery with her in his heart." By thwarting pornographic hungers, applicable to women

---

58. Oral Law # 102, based on Leviticus 18:20.

equally, whether visually or mediatorially through social media, all who submit to this infidelity confront the very reproving Son of Man.

Second, Jesus unilaterally ruled divorce activity inadmissible. Luke 16:18; Matthew 5:31–32, "It was also said, 'Whoever divorces his wife, let him give her a certificate of divorce.'[59] But I say to you that everyone who divorces his wife, except on the ground of sexual immorality, makes her commit adultery, and whoever marries a divorced woman commits adultery." Pharisaic/Sadduceic permissiveness relative to divorce was based on misinterpreting Deuteronomy 24:1–4. Jesus, in fact, stressed marriage's longevity. Mark 10:9; Matthew 19:6, "Whatever God has joined together, let not man separate." Thus, all whom Jesus binds together in holy matrimony, no covetousness, no government legislation, no code of law, and no court of public opinion may overturn or disqualify. Bonds of wedlock last as long as the man and the woman live, Romans 7:1–3.

Apostle Paul followed the Lord Jesus by teaching the hope of marital longevity. First Corinthians 7:10–11, "To the married I give this charge (not I, but the Lord): the wife should not separate from her husband (but if she does, she should remain unmarried or else be reconciled to her husband), and the husband should not divorce his wife." The Apostle's *moral oughts* integrated perfectly with Jesus' rulings on sexual morality.

Third, the Lord Jesus clearly revealed the indisputable foundation of the marriage institution. Mark 10:2–9; Matthew 19:3–9,

> And Pharisees came up to him and tested him by asking, "Is it lawful to divorce one's wife for any cause?" He answered, "Have you not read that he who created them from the beginning made them male and female, and said, 'Therefore a man shall leave his father and his mother and hold fast to his wife, and the two shall become one flesh'? So they are no longer two but one flesh. What therefore God has joined together, let not man separate." They said to him, "Why then did Moses command one to give a certificate of divorce and to send her away?" He said to them, "Because of your hardness of heart Moses allowed you to divorce your wives, but from the beginning it was not so. And I say to you: whoever divorces his wife, except for sexual immorality, and marries another, commits adultery."

A man and a woman joined by sexual intimacies know that the copulatory bond lasts as long as both shall live and, encircled by the adaptabilities of love, mature within this salutary marriage pledge. Ephesians 5:21–33; Colossians 3:18–19.

---

59. Oral Law # 77.

In every marital Christ-bond, headship never degenerates into violence and submission never slips into servitude. Hebrews' inspired author, 13:4, intensified this institution, "Let marriage be held in honor among all, and let the marriage bed be undefiled, for God will judge the sexually immoral and adulterous." Apostle Peter, therefore, in his first letter, 3:1–2, commanded, "Likewise, wives, be subject to your own husband, so that even if some do not obey the word, they may be won without a word by the conduct of their wives, when they see your respectful and pure conduct." And 1 Peter 3:7, "Likewise, husbands, live with your wives in an understanding way, showing honor to the woman as the weaker vessel,[60] since they are heirs with you of the grace of life, so that your prayers may not be hindered." Actually from Genesis throughout the New Testament, Jesus willed and wills covetous-free sexuality.

Also, Paul humanized procreation's sense. Colossians 3:20–21; Ephesians 6:1–4, "Children, obey your parents in the Lord, for this is right. 'Honor your father and mother'(this is the first commandment with a promise), 'that it may go well with you and that you may live long in the land.' Fathers, do not provoke your children to anger, but bring them up in the discipline and instruction of the Lord." Such coordinated family life, children obeying parents and parents obeying the Lord Jesus, ennobles sons and daughters generation upon generation.

In many ways, apostles as apostles build on the foundation of marital wisdom; working in the churches and on mission fields, they confronted every situation, then commanded husbands and wives to faithfulness. With respect to the women, 1 Timothy 2:9–10; 1 Peter 3:3–6, "Do not let your adorning be external—the braiding of hair and the putting on of gold jewelry, or the clothing you wear—but let your adorning be the hidden person of the heart with the imperishable beauty of a gentle and quiet spirit, which in God's sight is very precious. For this is how the holy women who hoped in God used to adorn themselves, by submitting to their own husbands, as Sarah obeyed Abraham, calling him lord.[61] And you are her children, if you do good and do not fear anything that is frightening." Every way to honor and promote marriage magnifies the Christ. For the Lord and Savior curbs every roaming sexual deceit with severest condemnation.

Thus, for the sake of the sanctity and sanity of wedlock, the culture within which marriage lives must be holy too. Ephesians 5:3–6; Colossians 3:5–6, "Put to death therefore what is earthly in you: sexual immorality,

---

60. The "weaker vessel" interprets Genesis 2:18, ". . . the LORD said, 'It is not good that the man should be alone. I will make him a helper fit for him.'"

61. Genesis 18:12.

impurity, passion, evil desire, and covetousness, which is idolatry. On account of these the wrath of God is coming." Sexual immoralities destructive of marital fidelity include homosexuality, lesbianism, transgenderism, prostitution, adultery, incest,[62] indeed, all fornicative contaminants.

By means of authoritative wisdom sayings, parables, and teachings (on human sexuality), all sharp as knives, Jesus separated Israel into distinct segments, since not all Israel is Israel.[63] As the Teacher, he prepared the New Church, the impactful evidence of the Kingdom, for the history of the second dispensation, his rule incontrovertible.

Healing Criteria

The Lord and Savior in his ministry healed the sick and the broken, exorcized demons, and resurrected dead people. Through his human voice of command, he displayed awesome divine powers. Every such miracle reflected his life-giving divinity. As the Author of life,[64] he healed, exorcised, and resurrected.

And oftentimes, Israelites praised Jesus for his teachings and healings; they sought out the evidence of his divinity—Matthew 4:23-25, 7:28-29, 8:14-17; Mark 1:29-34, 2:12, 3:7-12; Luke 4:14-15, 4:36-37, 38-41, 5:15, 26; John 7:21; Acts 3:10; etc. Upon evidential proof of his divinity, great praises engulfed the Lord and Savior.

1

At times, he granted health to multiple Israelites. Matthew 4:23-25. Matthew 8:16-17; Mark 1:32-34; Luke 4:40-41. Luke 5:15-16. Matthew 11:4-5; Luke 7:21. Mark 3:7-12; Luke 6:17-19. Matthew 12:15-21,

> Jesus . . . withdrew from there. And many followed him, and he healed them all and ordered them not to make him known. This was to fulfill what was spoken by the prophet Isaiah:

62. First Corinthians 5:1-5.

63. This separation stands out in believing and living the Faith, the latter Romans 12:1—15:13; 1 Corinthians 5:9-13, 12:1—14:25; Galatians 5:1-15; Ephesians 5:1-21; etc.

64. Norris. *Sources of Early Christian Thought: The Christological Controversy,* 89, "For this reason the things proper to this flesh are said to belong to him because he was in it—such things as being hungry, being thirsty, suffering, getting tired, and the like, to which the flesh is susceptible. But the proper works of the Logos himself, such as raising the dead and making the blind see and healing the woman with a hemorrhage, he accomplished through the instrumentality of his own body."

> "Behold, my servant whom I have chosen,
> my beloved with whom my soul is well pleased.
> I will put my Spirit upon him,
> and he will proclaim justice to the Gentiles.
> He will not quarrel or cry aloud,
> nor will anyone hear his voice in the street;
> a bruised reed he will not break,
> and a smoldering wick he will not quench,
> until he brings justice to victory;
> and in his name the Gentiles will hope."
> Isaiah 42:1–3

From there, the Synoptics moved on: Matthew 14:34–36; Mark 6:53–56. Matthew 15:29–31,

> Jesus . . . walked beside the Sea of Galilee. And he went up on the mountain and sat down there. And great crowds came to him, bringing with them the lame, the blind, the crippled, the mute, and many others, and they put them at his feet, and he healed them, so that the crowd wondered, when they saw the mute speaking, the crippled healthy, the lame walking, and the blind seeing. And they glorified [Jesus].

Unceasingly and omnipotently, Jesus, the God of Israel, healed on an unprecedented scale all brought to him, the presence of his divinity apparent. The antagonistic Pharisees found these people, measured by the Oral Law, the accursed and ignorant, John 7:49.

At other times, he granted renewal of life to individuals, one of whom a leper. Matthew 8:1–4; Mark 1:40–45; Luke 5:12–16. "While he was in one of the cities, there came a man full of leprosy. And when he saw Jesus, he fell on his face and begged him, 'Lord, if you will, you can make me clean.' And Jesus stretched out his hand and touched him,[65] saying, 'I will; be clean.' And immediately the leprosy left him. And he charged him to tell no one, but 'go and show yourself to the priest, and make an offering for your cleansing, as Moses commanded, for a proof to them.'" Further, Mark 7:31–37. Luke 7:1–10. Similarly, Matthew 8:5–13; also Peter's mother-in-law, Matthew 8:14–15; Mark 1:30–31; Luke 4:38–39. John, 4:46–54, 5:1–15, recorded other individual healings. Remarkably, Apostle John attended at length to the healing of a man born blind, John 9:1–41, whom Jesus cured, leaving the *seeing* Pharisees to their sightlessness.

On one occasion, he healed a paralytic; in the breathless moment, he revealed both his authority to rebuild the man's body and to pardon sin,

---

65. To prevent contagion, a severely forbidden gesture, Numbers 5:1–4.

Matthew 9:1-8; Mark 2:1-12; Luke 5:17-26, specifically 5:24, "But that you may know that the Son of Man has authority on earth to forgive sins"—he said to the man who was paralyzed—"I say to you, rise, pick up your bed and go home." With this miracle, Jesus highlighted the power dynamics of the Incarnation as well as the Crucifixion. He restored to health a woman who had only touched his clothing, Matthew 9:20-22; Mark 5:25-34; Luke 8:43-48. As recounted in Matthew 9:27-31, the Lord gave sight to two blind men. Matthew, 20:29-34, recorded the healing of two blind men; according to the same account, Mark, 10:46-53, and Luke, 18:35-43, narrated the eye-healing of one man.

Sabbath healings raised imperious Pharisaic ire. When Jesus restored a man's withered hand, menacing synagogue rulers fired up persecutory plans, Matthew 12:9-14; Mark 3:1-6; Luke 6:6-11. John 5:1-17, 18, 9:1-41 bared more of this overbearing resentment. Luke disseminated other instances of Sabbath healings, 14:1-6, 17:11-19, 18:35-43. Nevertheless, the Lord of the Sabbath, Matthew 12:1-8; Mark 2:23-28; Luke 6:1-5, since Genesis 2:1-3 planned the healing purpose of Seventh Days, pushing aside revolutionizing Oral Law directives.

With such healing capacities, the ascended and ruling Jesus empowered Peter and John, Acts 3:1-10; Stephen, Acts 6:8; Philip, Acts 8:7; Peter, Acts 5:12-16, 9:32-35, 12:6-11; Ananias, Acts 9:17; and Paul, Acts 14:8-10, 19:11-12, 28:1-6, 7-10, each life-giving act enforcing the recreative Gospel proclamation.

These healings, in multiples and in singles, gave historical evidence for Jesus' restorative work, to give life.

2

Jesus cleansed demon-possessed individuals, exceptionally so. With such afflictions, Satan contested the Lord and Savior's ministry. The Lord and Savior drew these possessed people to him for healing, taking away the Devil's controlling interests, Mark 1:21-28; Luke 4:31-37. Despite the Serpent's powers pressed to extreme limits, Jesus, without a trace of triumphalism, taught him in heartening moments of victory the impending end to his delusions. Matthew 12:28,

> ... if it is by the Spirit of God that I cast out demons, then the kingdom of God has come upon you.

Throughout the ministry years, Jesus by means of his humanity/divinity remained the superior, the Redeemer Lord.

At one point, Jesus with the disciples purposefully crossed the Sea of Galilee, or the Sea of Tiberias, to exorcise men, strangers to Israel, Gadarenes or Gerasenes, Matthew 8:28–34. Mark with more detail, 5:1–20, and Luke, 8:26–39, recorded the curing of one man, named Legion. Again, Matthew, 9:32–34, and Luke, 11:14, documented the exorcising of a mute, to the amazement of bystanders. Also, Jesus cast a demon out of the daughter of a Canaanite/Syrophoenician mother, Matthew 15:21–28; Mark 7:24–30. And the Synoptics chronicle the brief account of a young man's recovery from demon-possession, Matthew 17:14–20; Mark 9:14–29; Luke 9:37–43.

The Lord Jesus enabled Philip, Acts 8:7, and Paul, Acts 16:16–18, 19:11–12, to exorcise demon possession.

As the Lord Jesus drew these *psychotic* people into his presence, Israelites as well as Gentiles, he removed them, person by person, from the Satan's clandestine wheels of power, signaling thereby the coming Crucifixion victory.

3

Jesus commanded various resurrections, thereby revealing ultimate authority. In the Old Testament dispensation, he had demonstrated this benefaction through Elijah, 1 Kings 17:17–24, and Elisha, 2 Kings 4:32–37, 13:20–21. Directly, he called Jairus' daughter to life, Matthew 9:18–26; Mark 5:35–43; Luke 8:49–56. He also raised up a widow's son, Luke 7:11–17. In an impressive display of decisive authority, he summoned four-days-dead Lazarus out of a tomb, John 11:38–44. Then with his final breath, dying, he opened tombs in and about Jerusalem; many deceased came back to life, Matthew 27:52–53. These resurrections proved Jesus' mastery over the last enemy.

As Peter and Paul entered upon respective ministries, the Lord Jesus granted each extremes of healing; Peter raised Dorcas/Tabitha from the sleep of death, Acts 9:36–43, and Paul dead Eutychus, Acts 20:7–12. These resurrections proved the Resurrection's actuality. For, 1 Corinthians 15:13, ". . . if there is no resurrection of the dead, then not even Christ has been raised."

Now, three summary statements with respect to Jesus' exulting authority manifested through his humanity:

Two bread-and-fish miracles, Matthew 14:13–21; Mark 6:30–44; Luke 9:10–17; John 6:1–14, and Matthew 15:32–38, as all signs and wonders, constituted life-giving works. Jesus according to Apostle John's version of the feeding of 5,000, made this the basis for a sacrament, John 6:52-59, in this manner opening up deep Passover dimensions.

Collectively these healings, exorcisms, and resurrections displayed the Lord and Savior's exalting authority over life and death, power active even in the very hour of his Crucifixion. Without in the Pharisee-manner demanding compensation, he freely created physical, mental, and emotional recoveries without charging a denarius and without demanding reciprocity. He gave life and gave liberally, magnified as eternal life, John 17:2-3.

Over Jesus' three years of ruling, infuriated Israelite leadership more intensely plotted his murder; mercilessly, they intended to kill him and obliterate the Gospel, which superseded by far the fraudulence of Pharisaism/Sadduceism. Yet majestically, through his human voice of command, he displayed awesomely divine powers. Thus, in every day of ministry, Jesus humbly and majestically revealed the exaltation of his divinity.

Jesus' Humiliation

Jesus, the Man,[66] in the very pit of humiliation created the Atonement. Commissioned by God the Father's blessing, moved by the indwelling Holy Spirit, and compelled by his divinity, the Man bore the punishment for the immeasurable guilt his people grossed and gross on account of disobeying the Gospel and therewith the Law.[67] This great grace originated beyond capabilities of human understanding; its unmerited mercy forever the Church's salting salt.

1

Out of the Jewish world, vilifiers attacked Jesus progressing into the Expiation. Actually, this humiliation of Jesus' humanity started in and with the Incarnation,[68] Philippians 2:5-8; when the omnipresent God the Son *emptied himself* of celestial glory (a metaphor expressing the inexpressible), he surrendered his resplendent essence and eternal form (*morphe*) of divinity by bonding with the crucial and temporal form (*schema*) of a man. With and in this humanity, at all times surrounded by and filled with his divinity,

---

66. John 19:5, "Behold the man!"

67. John 1:9-11, "The true light, which enlightens everyone, was coming into [Israel]. He was in [Israel], and [Israel] was made through him, yet [Israel] did not know him. He came to his own, and his own people did not receive him."

68. Throughout preincarnate ages, God the Father prepared God the Son by way of servant prophecies as Isaiah 49:5-6, 52:13—53:12; etc.

he bore the indescribably measureless burdens of moral guilt. Hence, in and since the Incarnation, Jesus bared his humanity to extremes of vilification.[69]

By eternally binding his divinity to his humanity, God the Son with God the Father and God the Spirit created the Jesus forever immortalized in John 1:14, "And the Word became[70] flesh and dwelt among us, and we have seen his glory, glory as of the only Son from the Father, full of grace and truth." With his humanity God the Son, now the Son of God, walked the way of humiliation from Galilee over Jerusalem onto Golgotha, the place of execution outside the City of the great King, Hebrews 13:12. Jesus' divinity with all omnipotence and omniscience moved his humanity down most drastic levels of degradation and disgrace to its sacrifice. Over three years, the Pharisees brimming with hatred,[71] aided by the Sadducees bursting with hostility, and abetted by Caesarian Romans teeming with enmity, plotted the death of the Man, Matthew 26:3–5, thereby *assisting* in creating the Atonement. Acts 2:22–23,

> ... hear these words: Jesus of Nazareth, a man attested to you by God with mighty works and wonders and signs that God did through him in your midst, as you yourselves know—this Jesus, delivered up according to the definite plan and foreknowledge of God, you crucified and killed by the hands of lawless men.

The eternal binding of divinity and humanity opened Jesus to incalculable horrors of dehumanizing despair.

To define this humiliation on one level, John the Baptizer had classified Jesus' enemies a brood of vipers, Luke 3:7; Matthew 3:7. This character assessment stigmatized the Pharisee menace, the Sadducee hostility, and the Serpent, the unforgiveable sinner. Unable and unwilling to recognize Jesus' divinity, they went after his humanity, seeking its obliteration. The Serpent/Devil first attempted to humiliate Jesus by tempting his humanity with his own possessions, the kingdoms of the world, were he to give up

---

69. Rush. *Sources of Early Christian Thought: The Christological Controversy*, 90, "Consequently, when the flesh was suffering, the Logos was not apart from it. That is why the suffering also is said to belong to him."
Philippians 2:8, "And being found in human form, he humbled himself by becoming obedient to the point death, even death on a cross."
Hebrews 5:8, "Although he was a son, he learned obedience through what he suffered."

70. White. *The Forgotten Trinity*, 56, "Here John uses *egeneto*, a verb that refers to an action in time. And the reason is clear: the Word entered into human existence, 'became flesh,' at a particular point in time."

71. Acts 7:51a, "You stiff-necked people, uncircumcised in heart and ears, you always resist the Holy Spirit."

on the Atonement, Matthew 4:1–11; Luke 4:1–13. Failing, the shamed and spiteful Tempter personally directed his Pharisee/Sadducee proxies, from within Israel, John 8:44, empowering them to entice Jesus to abandon the road to Golgotha and alienate himself from the way of redemption.

On another level, after a healing miracle, the temporizing Jews had had enough. Blind to Jesus' divinity and therefore unable to appreciate his works as heaven-generated miracles, they tyrannously conspired at homicide, Matthew 12:14; Luke 6:11; Mark 3:6, "The Pharisees went out and immediately held counsel with the Herodians against [Jesus], how to destroy him." This monumental upwelling of hatred approached spontaneous combustion. Matthew 26:3–5; Mark 12:12; Luke 20:19–20, "The scribes and the chief priests sought to lay hands on him at that very hour, for they perceived that he had told [the Parable of the Wicked Tenants] against them, but they feared the people. So they watched him and sent spies, who pretended to be sincere, that they might catch him in something he said, so to deliver him up to the authority and jurisdiction of the governor." Lastly and desperately, by night and by Judas, a mob armed with swords and clubs *captured* the Son of God. Matthew 26:47–56; Mark 14:43–50; Luke 22:47–53; John 18:2–11. At this point in time, the Pharisee/Sadducee abhorrence of the Christ broke out in the infamous rant, "Crucify him!" Scriptures' Author/authors engraved this tirade of religiosity, the Serpent's final attempt to force Jesus away from the Atonement, explicitly and eternally into the New Church's soul, unforgettably; the hatred ballooned with the totality of satanic loathing and burst with all its violence over Jesus' head, therewith to twist and turn the Man cruelly from fulfilling his ministry of grace and mercy.

2

Jesus actively embodied this burgeoning revulsion of hatred in his humanity; sacrificially, he submitted his physicality, mentality, and emotionality, the standard features of every man, to the ravages of animosity.

To be sure of his humanity, a brief oversight suffices. Physically, he experienced hunger, Matthew 4:2; Hebrews 2:27; fatigue, Mark 3:5; John 4:6; sleep, Mark 4:38, and thirst, John 4:7, 19:28. Intellectually, he received a typical Jewish education, Luke 2:46, 52, and at maturity possessed a normally accumulating library of thoughts, reflections, and memories, a mind energetically at work. And emotionally, he knew the full range of human sentiment—love, John 15:12; sorrow, John 11:35; anger, Mark 3:5; John 2:13–22; Matthew 21:12–17; Mark 11:15–19; Luke 19:45–45; temptation, Matthew 4:1–11; Luke 4:1–13; marvel, Mark 6:6; Matthew 8:10; Luke 7:9;

sympathy, Hebrews 10:32-34; grief. Mark 3:5; compassion, Mark 6:34; frustration/sighing, Mark 7:34, 8:12; indignation, Mark 10:14—that testifies to normal humanity. Hebrews 2:17, ". . . he had to be made like his brothers in every respect, so that he might become a merciful and faithful high priest in the service of God, to make propitiation for the sins of the people." In his full and total humanity, Jesus unsparingly yielded to the sufferings of hatred.

Hence, at age 30, he perfectly executed his own standard of excellence. Leviticus 19:2b, "You shall be holy, for I the LORD your God am holy." Tempered by his sanctity, the Son of God—consciously and knowingly—walked the Crucifixion-road from Bethlehem to Jerusalem, taking in flaring pains of rejection. Informed by his divinity's omniscience, he was always aware of the malign plotting to repudiate his ministry and forestall the Gospel, knowing that more suffering of body, mind, and soul awaited him in every tomorrow. Nevertheless, he pressed on, even if perceived an interloper in the claustrophobic realms of the Pharisee, Sadducee, and Roman religiosities.

Without overlooking its excruciating impact, Peter's denial of knowing him, the Christ, cut to the quick, Matthew 26:30-35, 69-75; Mark 14:27-31, 66-72; Luke 22:31-34, 54-62; John 13:36-38, 18:15-18, 25-37. This disciple's rejection, more than the others' escape from the arresting mob, Mark 14:51-52; Matthew 26:56p, measured the Lord and Savior's aloneness: alone he faced the expiatory terrors of hell, the worst of the Serpent's inflictions.

At a decisive moment, deep in the Jewish soul, a life-eating malignity decided to overcome the destruction of the rebelliously restless Israelite nation by Roman overmight; through offering up the life of one man, John 11:49-51, 18:14, the leaders accomplished this "salvation." And the Pharisee/Sadducee strategy for survival, combined with Roman collaboration, worked; they pushed and pulled Jesus Cross-ward. Instead of Israel suffering loss, the Son of God knew in the agonies of rejection on the Cross the hellish pains of the representative expiation.

By stealth and by night, Jesus' enemies in the grip of the Enemy made the Man's capture happen, Mark 14:1-2; Luke 22:1-2; Matthew 26:3-5, 47-56, "according to the definite plan and foreknowledge of [God the Father]," Acts 2:23p. Slyly, Israel's movers and shakers refused to look once more into the gaping abyss of damnation; the Man had to go, a small price for saving the peoples of the Pharisee and the Sadducee religiosities.

In Jesus' humiliation, John 14:28p gains clarity, ". . . for the Father is greater than I." In divinity and glory, God the Son equals God the Father. The comparison applies to God the Father in relation to Jesus' humanity. This humanity—planned by God the Father, enlivened by God the Spirit, and enveloped by God the Son's omnipresence—became the sacrificial Man totally humiliated, humiliation begun with the Incarnation.

3

Pharisee/Sadducee acrimony boiled over at the bizarre trial; on the basis of false accusation, blasphemy, Luke 22:71, Mark 14:64; Matthew 26:65, and because of misunderstood truth, kingship, John 18:37, the Sanhedrin and Pontius Pilate condemned Jesus' humanity to the pit of humiliation, a humiliation aggravated by Barabbas' release, Matthew 27:15–23. When the Roman governor had discovered in Jesus nothing worthy of the death penalty, except perhaps the claim to Caesar's throne, the uproarious "Crucify him!" recorded as Matthew 27:22b; Mark 15:13–14; Luke 23:23; John 19:6 *persuaded* the man to release a criminal and crucify the Son of Man. What did he care for a despised Jew hated most intensely by his own people?

Throughout the expiatory—that is, the cleansing from sin—Crucifixion,[72] Jesus' humiliation reached its ultimate nadir:

One. The Pharisee/Sadducee mockeries invoked the self-condemnatory language of reprobation, John 19:17–22; Luke 23:32–43; Mark 15:21–32; Matthew 27:32–44; this derision, as Matthew recorded, spelled out the Serpent's anguish. From passers-by, "You who would destroy the temple and rebuild it in three days, save yourself! If you are the Son of God, come down from the cross." And from present chief priests, scribes, and elders, "He who saved others, he cannot save himself. He is the King of Israel; let him come down now from the cross, and we will believe in him. He trusts in [the Father, whom Jesus professed]; let God deliver him now, if he desires him. For he said, 'I am the Son of God.'" The blasphemers continued, desperate to save perilous religiosities, and *prove* the Serpent's superiority.

Two. For the detachment of Roman soldiers charged with the crucifixion, Jesus' death eliminated only one more scorned Jew; throughout this routine execution, they had no eye for the Savior of the world.[73]

Three. In the terrifying darkness, Jesus, despairingly, cried out the cry of dereliction—"Eli, Eli, lama sabachthani?"—that symbolized God the Father's rejection of his humanity. This wail erupted from the deepest depths of his hellish agony. He had reached the Hades of ultimate desolation and anguish. In that hour, his humanity no longer recognized the significance of the Incarnation, its divine-human bonding, and its hitherto tenacity to stay the course.

---

72. Argyle. *God in the New Testament*, 18, "In so far as the concept of sacrifice is applied by New Testament writers to the Crucifixion of Jesus, the self-offering of Christ in obedience to the will of God, it is viewed chiefly under its expiatory aspect, as a cleansing from sin and guilt, and thus a means of reconciliation between the sinner and God."

73. The centurion in command of the crucifying detail found Jesus innocent, Luke 23:47; according to Mark 15:39, this same centurion called Jesus a son of a Roman god.

In that deepest of torments, inexpressible and immeasurable, Jesus' divinity strengthened his humanity to make the Atonement.

The dominical Lord and Savior had visualized the measureless peril of suffering by transforming the Passover celebration into the Lord's Supper, he the Lamb, Isaiah 53:7; Luke 22:14–23; Matthew 26:26–29; Mark 14:17–25. The institutionalized Passover commemorates the Gospel visibly and palpably. Thus First Corinthians 11:23–26,

> For I received from the Lord what I also delivered to you, that the Lord Jesus on the night when he was betrayed took bread, and when he had given thanks, he broke it, and said, "This is my body which is for you. Do this in remembrance of me." In the same way also he took the cup, after supper, saying, "This cup is the new covenant in my blood. Do this, as often as you drink it, in remembrance of me." For as often as you eat this bread and drink the cup, you proclaim the Lord's death until he comes.

In this manner, Apostle Paul *portrayed* the sacrament Jesus had instituted in order that the Church, remembering, internalizes the transaction in the Crucifixion—his life for the believers.'

Apostle John, with most illuminating analogy, presented Jesus' human body and blood as the bread and drink for eternal life; 6:54–55, "Whoever feeds on my flesh and drinks my blood has eternal life, and I will raise him up on the last day. For my flesh is true food, and my blood is true drink." Thus the Lamb, full of grace and truth, gave his humanity, the once-for-all sacrifice, Hebrews 10:10.

To achieve the Atonement, the Lord and Savior had taken the offensive, stirring about in Pharisee and Sadducee religiosity, as well as at the end in the Roman; he made the hostility of the people public. With respect to one, he revealed that that Jewish idolatry never represented the soul of the Kingdom/Recreation and, with respect to the other, that the Roman Empire's pantheon represented the soul of the world.

Jesus' Glorification

Away from human perception,
outside the range of human comprehension,
behind the stone enclosing the sepulcher,
the Trinity resurrected Jesus' humanity,
imperceptibly.
The Serpent,

> dominating by death,
> lost,
> his head crushed.
>
> Death is swallowed up in victory.
> O death, where is your victory?
> O death, where is your sting?
> Hosea 13:14b/1 Corinthians 15:54–55

Upon Jesus' exiting from his tomb, his humanity resurrected, the Three-in-One disclosed the glories of his experienced transformation, John 17:5. Scriptures' Author/authors revealed that Jesus, the King of kings and Lord of lords, according to his recreated humanity and in divine omnipotence, omniscience, and omnipresence, strode onto the ground of his supremacy, the Church the foremost evidence of the Kingdom/Recreation.

1

Jesus' transformed humanity opened in its impressive recreation[74]—free in immortality, free in sensibility, free in movement, and free in the joy of the Atonement with as many as God the Father had appointed for eternal life.

Upon completing the substitutionary atonement, the Resurrection freed the Lord and Savior from further carrying measureless burdens of guilt that had weighed upon his humanity, as celebrated in the Lord's Supper, Matthew 26:26–29; Mark 14:22–25; Luke 22:19–24; 1 Corinthians 10:14—22, 11:17–34. Walking now erect, he moved highly exalted to his rightful seat of authority, God the Father next to him affirming that this Jesus, this Jesus seated beside him, governed the universe, even the lot of every newly conceived child.

As the First-born of the Kingdom/Recreation, Colossians 1:15, Jesus imputed to his people the Spirit's love of life—life in the age to come now unfolding in every congregation, family, and person. And, maximally, with his eternally conjoined humanity and divinity, he works consequent victories over sin, Satan, and submission to decay, Acts 2:31. In every way, all beneficiaries of Jesus' magnification hope for the Consummation presented in Revelation 21:5, "Behold, I am making all things new."

---

74. Poythress. *The Mystery of the Trinity,* 11, "The resurrection involves the transformation of Christ's body from death to life."

2

With majestic ease, Jesus moved his humanity for locality to locality; without removing the stone-door blocking the sepulcher's exit, he, resurrected, strode forth. Matthew 28:1–10,

> Now after the Sabbath, toward the dawn of the first day of the week, Mary Magdalene and the other Mary went to see the tomb. And behold, there was a great earthquake, for an angel of the Lord descended from heaven and came and rolled back the stone and sat on it. His appearance was like lightning, and his clothing white as snow. And for fear of him the guards trembled and became like dead men. But the angel said to the women, "Do not be afraid, for I know that you seek Jesus who was crucified. He is not here, for he has risen, as he said. Come, see the place where he lay. Then go quickly and tell his disciples that he has risen from the dead, and behold, he is going before you to Galilee; there you will see him. See, I have told you." So they departed quickly from the tomb with fear and great joy, and ran to tell the disciples. And behold, Jesus met them and said, "Greetings!" And they came up and took hold of his feet and worshiped him. Then Jesus said to them, "Do not be afraid; go and tell my brothers to go to Galilee, and there they will see me."

Other than incidental differences, Mark, 16:1–8, Luke, 24:1–12, and John, 20:1–10 confirmed the same reality; with his glorified humanity, Jesus moved at will between heaven and earth, and in the earth without attention to physical barriers.

3

At the *intersection* of the Trinity's omnipotence, omniscience, and omnipresence, the invisible Three-of-the-Divinity recreated Jesus' humanity. Yet, upon the transformation, his followers recognized him, Luke 24:36–43, John 20:11–23, even touched him, John 20:11–18, 18–23, 26–29; 1 John 1:1–3. The same Jesus who had died most humiliatingly appeared gloriously at the center of the budding Church.

With similar effortlessness, Jesus appeared to and disappeared from the two Emmaus-bound men, Luke 24:15, 31. Because of his transformed humanity, time/space obstacles no longer limited him to Jerusalem, even Canaan; now in and with his humanity bonded to his divinity, he moved freely between heaven and earth.

4

Frequently, Scriptures attest to God the Father's involvement in the Resurrection, validating its actuality.

> Psalm 16:10/Acts 2:24, "God raised him up, loosing the pangs of death, because it was not possible for him to be held by it."
>
> Psalm 49:15/Acts 2:30–32, "Being therefore a prophet, and knowing that God has sworn with an oath to [David] that he would set one of his descendants on his throne, he foresaw and spoke about the resurrection of the Christ, that he was not abandoned to Hades, nor did his flesh see corruption."
>
> John 5:21, "For as the Father raises the dead and gives them life, so also the Son gives life to whom he will."
>
> Acts 2:32, "This Jesus God raised up, and of that we all are witnesses."
>
> Acts 2:36, "Let all the house of Israel therefore know for certain that God has made him both Lord and Christ, this Jesus whom you crucified."
>
> Acts 3:13, "The God of Abraham, the God of Isaac, and the God of Jacob, the God of our fathers, glorified his servant[75] Jesus, whom you delivered over and denied in the presence of Pilate, when he had decided to release him." Acts 7:32; Matthew 22:32; Luke 20:37.
>
> Acts 3:15a, "... you killed the Author of life, whom God raised from the dead."
>
> Acts 3:26, "God, having raised up his servant, sent him to you first, to bless you by turning every one of you from your wickedness."
>
> Acts 5:31,13:30; Romans 6:4; 1 Corinthians 15:1–11; Ephesians 1:19–20; 1 Peter 1:21.
>
> Etc.

In eternity, God the Father planned the requisites for the Resurrection and with omnipotent authority summoned Jesus out of the last enemy's stranglehold.

---

75. Servant refers to Jesus' humanity.

Jesus testified to his rightful authority over death. In the Old Testament dispensation, he overcame death through Elijah, 1 Kings 17:21-22, and Elisha, 2 Kings 4:32-35, 13:20-21. Through his ministry in Israel, he resurrected several covenant people: Jairus' daughter, Matthew 9:18-26; Mark 5:35-43, a widow's son, Luke 7:11-17, and Lazarus, John 11:38-44. Then, by way of apostles, he restored Dorcas/Tabitha to life, Acts 9:36-43, and Eutychus, Acts 20:9-12. Also, Jesus directly affirmed his authority over death.

John 2:19, "Destroy this temple, and in three days I will raise it up."

John 5:21, 25, "Truly, truly, an hour is coming, and is now here, when the dead will hear the voice of the Son of God, and those who hear will live."

Daniel 12:2/John 5:28-29, "Do not marvel at this, for an hour is coming when all who are in the tombs will hear his voice and come out, those who have done good to the resurrection of life, and those who have done evil to the resurrection of judgment."

John 6:39-40, 44, 54, 57, "As the living Father sent me, and I live because of the Father, so whoever feeds on me, he also will live because of me."

John 10:17-18, "For this reason the Father loves me, because I lay down my life that I make take it up again. No one takes it from me, but I lay it down of my own accord. I have authority to lay it down, and I have authority to take it up again."

John 11:25, "I am the resurrection and the life."

Etc.

Through Apostle Paul, he reconfirmed this authority, 1 Corinthians 15:53, "For this perishable body must put on the imperishable, and this mortal body must put on immortality." Thus Jesus with his divinity/humanity ruled over death, compelling Satan to surrender his pretentious and fraudulent claims over the Kingdom/Recreation's citizens.

The Three-of-the-Trinity with almighty acclaim transformed Jesus' humanity, living proof for that which happens to believers in the final resurrection of the dead.

5

Once, Jesus' humanity shone radiantly; for a brief moment in time, his temporarily transfigured manhood gave transitory evidence of eschatological glory. Matthew 17:1-13; Mark 9:2-13; Luke 9:28-36, ". . . the appearance of his face was altered, and his clothing became dazzling white." Something less spectacular occurred to Moses[76] and Elijah[77] who spoke with Jesus to fortify him for the ultimate humiliation, the representative atonement. The transfiguration of Jesus' humanity prepared him for glories centering in post-Crucifixion radiances.

6

On Resurrection Day, according to John 8:21, 12:32; Luke 24:50-53, Jesus in the presence of his disciples/apostles physically ascended into the omnipresence of the Divinity.

> Then he led them out as far as Bethany, and lifting up his hands he blessed them. While he blessed them, he parted from them and was carried up into heaven. And they worshiped him and returned to Jerusalem with great joy, and were continually in the temple blessing God.

Forty days later, after meeting with the disciples numerous times and teaching them about the Kingdom/Recreation, Jesus ascended with finality, his humanity to remain in the heavens until the conclusion to the second dispensation. Acts 1:9-11,

> . . . as the [Twelve] were looking on, [Jesus] was lifted up, and a cloud took him out of their sight. And while they were gazing into heaven as he went, behold, two men stood by them in white robes, and said, "Men of Galilee, why do you stand looking into heaven? This Jesus, who was taken up from you into heaven, will come in the same way as you saw him go into heaven."

---

76. Exodus 34:29-33; 2 Corinthians 3:12-18.

77. After freeing Israel from Egyptian captivity, the Lord God interred Moses, Deuteronomy 34:5-6, and after liberating Northern Israel from Baalism, the Lord had Elijah ascend in spectacular fashion, 2 Kings 2:11. Both prophets *saw* the Preincarnate, Exodus 33:19-23; 1 Kings 19:9-13. On the Mount of Transfiguration they spoke with him.

Thus, as reputable witnesses testified, Jesus' humanity *disappeared* into the Trinity's omnipresence. With the Father and the Spirit, Jesus reigns over heaven and earth, his humanity too glorifying the Trinity.

7

Post-Resurrection, Jesus appeared to the Twelve. Luke 24:13–35 recorded the Lord's conversation with the two Emmaus-men; then, Luke 24:36, "As [the Twelve] were talking about these things, Jesus himself stood among them, and said to them, 'Peace to you.'" John, 20:19–29, 21:1–25, verified similar Christophanies, which he in his first letter summed up, 1:1–3,

> That which was from the beginning, which we have heard, which we have seen with our eyes, which we looked upon and have touched with our hands, concerning the word of life—the life was made manifest, and we have seen it, and testify to it and proclaim to you the eternal life, which was with the Father and was made manifest to us—that which we have seen and heard we proclaim also to you, so that you too may have fellowship with us; and indeed our fellowship is with the Father and with his Son Jesus Christ.

For the benefits of this ecclesiastical fellowship to come alive, Jesus ascended, John 8:14, 16:5, 7.

Upon the Ascension and Pentecost, Jesus appeared to select believers in the way of Christophanies.

> Acts 7:55–56, "But [Stephen], full of the Holy Spirit, gazed into heaven and saw the glory of God, and Jesus standing at the right hand of God. And he said, 'Behold, I see the heavens opened, and the Son of Man standing at the right hand of God.'"

> Acts 9:3–5, "Now as [Paul] went on his way, he approached Damascus, and suddenly a light from heaven flashed around him. And falling to the ground he heard a voice saying to him, 'Saul, Saul, why are you persecuting me?' And he said, 'Who are you, Lord?' And he said, 'I am Jesus, whom you are persecuting.'" Acts 26:13.

> Acts 10:9–16, Pete's vision of the great sheet filled with unclean animals, and Jesus saying, "Rise, Peter; kill and eat."

TRINITARIAN EXALTATION

In The Revelation, Apostle John presented Jesus, high and exalted, in lustrous portrayals. Given this book's seven sections,[78] he first envisioned Jesus' humanity with and in which he ruled the heavens and the earth for the sake of the Church as portrayed in immediate post-Ascension glory. The Apostle saw, Revelation 1:12-16,

> ... in the midst of the lampstands one like a son of man, clothed with a long robe and with a golden sash around his chest. The hairs of his head were white, like white wool, like snow. His eyes were like a flame of fire, his feet were like burnished bronze, refined in a furnace, and his voice was like the roar of many waters. In his right hand he held seven stars, from his mouth came a sharp two-edged sword, and his face was like the sun shining in full strength.

In the second section, 4-7, the Apostle revealed Jesus' humanity as the Lamb taking the scroll of rulership from God the Father's hand. Revelation 5:6-8.

In the third section, 8-11, again immediately upon the Ascension, the Lamb released the Serpent's riders on colored horses spreading destruction and death—to make unbelievers taste eternal destiny apart from Christ and to test believers preparatory to eternity in Christ.

In the fourth section, 12-14, John saw the Incarnation from heaven's point of view as well as the Serpent's major defeat.

In the fifth section, 15-16, the Christ's angels pour out preliminary evidence of the Serpent's subsequent routs, inclusive the overthrow at Armageddon. Second Peter 3:11-13 details his final collapse.

In the sixth section, 17-19, upon the conquest of Babylon/Rome, Jesus reveals himself as the Groom in the glory of the consummating marriage-feast, and as the King of kings and Lord of lords.

In the seventh section, 20-22, Jesus revealed his humanity by judging the nations, finally defeating the Serpent, presenting the glorious New Jerusalem, and crowning his now all-encompassing universal Kingdom/Recreation with glory. Revelation 21:33. Then the great trinitarian throne stands central forever and ever, Revelation 22:3.

Jesus, leading the Church further and farther toward the Eschaton, upon the Ascension portrayed his humanity. With each glorious portrayal, he revealed his victory on the Cross over abominable hellish agonies to merit the salvation of the Church. The Trinity resurrected him from the

---

78. Hendriksen. *More Than Conquerors*, 28, the seven divisions: 1-3, 4-7, 8-11, 12-14, 15-16, 17-19, 20-22. Note: each division begins where the Gospels leave off, approximately at the Ascension.

dead and in that glory, taking his transformed humanity up, placed him on the seat of authority at the right hand of God the Father, God the Father eternally testifying to his rulership. Second Corinthians 4:6, "For God, who said, 'Let light shine out of darkness,' has shone in our hearts to give the light of the knowledge of the glory of God in the face of Jesus Christ."

Now, to know the infallible and indissoluble interactions between Jesus' visible humanity and invisible divinity further solidifies knowing God the Son. Knowing God the Son actuates knowing God the Father in his ground planning for the Kingdom/Recreation and the Church's salvation, the whole of which God the Spirit animated with life.

God the Spirit's Exaltation

God the Spirit,[79] even as God the Father, in his workings magnified Jesus' humanity, John 16:14. He glorified him throughout the Incarnation, Matthew 1:20; Luke 1:35, and at his baptism, Matthew 3:13–17; Mark 1:9–11; Luke 3:21–22; John 1:32–34. In fact, since the beginning, God the Spirit magnified God the Son as well as God the Father. In the fullness of time, God the Father and God the Son[80] sent the Spirit.

John the Baptizer throughout the dynamics of ministry promised a baptism more decisive than immersion in running Jordan waters. Matthew 3:11, "I baptize you with water for repentance, but he who is coming after me is mightier than I . . . He will baptize you with the Holy Spirit and fire." To be sure, Jesus repeated this prophecy specifically to the Twelve, Acts 1:5. By this more relevant sacrament, the Lord and Savior created the New Church, her members blessed by the indwelling Spirit, Titus 3:5; 2 Peter 1:4.

To toughen Jesus' humanity for the atoning task ahead and the Serpent's final onslaught, the Spirit led him into a wilderness area about the Jordan in the Galilee region, there to confront the Archenemy, the malevolent Serpent most intense now to quash the Son of Man, lest he be forced into his

---

79. Smail, Thomas, "The Holy Spirit in the Holy Trinity," 149–65, in Seitz. *Nicene Christianity,* 152, "Jesus finishes his work and returns to the Father, but the Spirit leads his people in every generation into the unfolding riches and manifold implications of what he has done, and thus brings him new glory."

Owen. *The Holy Spirit,* 98, "By [Jesus] he was directed, comforted, and supported in the whole course of his ministry, temptations, obedience, and sufferings."

80. The *filioque* clarified that God the Father and God the Son sent the Spirit who upon Pentecost Day blessed the Kingdom/Recreation with eternal life.

Rusch. *Early Sources of Christian Thought: The Trinitarian Controversy,* 26, "For Augustine, the Spirit is the Spirit of both Father and Son."

ultimate demise. Matthew, 4:1–11, Mark, 1:12–13, and Luke, 4:1–13, record the conflict, Jesus the superior by quoting his Old Testament Scriptures.

The Spirit is the Helper Jesus promised, John 14:16, 16:13, the Spirit of truth, John 14:26, teaching and bringing to remembrance all that the Lord and Savior had taught. Jesus therefore sent him in his name and by God the Father's cooperation, to make the Church actually the Church, the witness to the truth of the Kingdom/Recreation as well as the Parousia, John 14:26, 15:26–27, 16:7–11. Thus the Spirit completes and complements Jesus' mission and motivates the people of the Church to glorify the Lord and Savior in his humanity and his divinity, indeed, to magnify the Trinity.

God the Spirit, yes, he is God, Matthew 28:19; Acts 5:3–4, inserted himself recreatively into Jesus' followers in order that they, too, even if caught up in persecution, confess the Lord and Savior's name. Matthew 10:20; Mark 13:11, "And when [my enemies] bring you to trial and deliver you over, do not be anxious beforehand what you are to say, but say whatever is given you in that hour, for it is not you who speak, but the Holy Spirit." Living in Christ valorizes the persecuted with a maturing illuminated in Romans 5:1–5.

At returning to Nazareth, resistance to Jesus' ministry erupted at his declaration of his unity in the Trinity, Matthew 13:53–58; Mark 6:1–6; Isaiah 61:1–2/Luke 4:18–19.

> The Spirit of the Lord is upon me,
> because he as anointed me to proclaim good news to the poor.
> He has sent me to proclaim liberty to the captives and recovering of sight to the blind,
> to set at liberty those who are oppressed,
> to proclaim the year of the Lord's favor.

At this full equivalence of Deity, the Nazareth synagogue claimed blasphemy, Leviticus 24:16, and sprang up in violence. Luke 4:16–30, "When they heard these things, all in the synagogue were filled with wrath. And they rose up and drove him out of the town and brought him to the brow of the hill on which their town was built, so that they could throw him down the hill." Though they attempted murder, this was not the Son of God's Golgotha-hour.

Jesus, exulting in ministry, unwrapped horrors for all who resisted and resist the Spirit's magnification of his humanity. Mark 3:28–30; Matthew 12:31–32, ". . . I tell you, every sin and blasphemy will be forgiven people, but the blasphemy against the Spirit will not be forgiven. And whoever speaks a word against the Son of Man will be forgiven, but whoever speaks against the Holy Spirit will not be forgiven, either in this age or in the age to come." Even in the midst of unforgiveable sinners, the Spirit innovates boldness in believers to confess the Faith, thus glorifying the Christ. John 12:36b–43 pointed out the fallacious powers of unfaithfulness.

> When Jesus had [spoken of the Crucifixion], he departed and hid himself from [Israelite enemies]. Though he had done so many signs before them, they still did not believe him, so that the word spoken by the prophet Isaiah might be fulfilled:
>
> > Lord, who has believed what he heard from us,
> > and to whom has the arm of the LORD been revealed?
> > Isaiah 53:1
>
> Therefore they could not believe. For again Isaiah said,
> He has blinded their eyes and hardened their heart,
> lest they see with their eyes,
> and understand with their heart,
> and turn
> and I would heal them.
> Isaiah 6:10
>
> Isaiah said these things because he saw [the Christ's] glory and spoke of him. Nevertheless, many even of the authorities believed in him, but for fear of the Pharisees they did not confess it, so that they would not be put out of the synagogue; for they loved the glory that comes from man more than the glory that comes from God.

Due to Israel's unfaithfulness, Jesus bypassed its multitudes in order to concentrate only on all whom God the Father entrusted to him; these turned to him and actually heard the Gospel. In this manner, he repudiated and slew the powers that rule this present world.

In the fourth Gospel, Apostle John innovatively related the Spirit's ministry by which God the Son ingathered all God the Father delegated to hear and believe him:

> John 3:8, "The wind blows where it wishes, and you hear its sound, but you do not know where it comes from or where it goes."
>
> John 6:63, "It is the Spirit who gives life; the flesh is no help at all."
>
> John 7:37b–38, "If anyone thirsts, let him come to me and drink. Whoever believes in me, as the Scripture has said, 'Out of his heart will flow rivers of living water.'"

John 14:15-17, "If you love me, you will keep my commandments. And I will ask the Father, and he will give you another Helper, to be with you forever, even the Spirit of truth, whom the world cannot receive, because it neither sees him nor knows him. You know him, for he dwells with you and will be in you."

John 14:26, "But the Helper, the Holy Spirit, whom the Father will send in my name, he will teach you all things and bring to your remembrance all that I have said to you."

John 15:26, "But when the Helper comes, whom I will send to you from the Father, the Spirit of truth, who proceeds from the Father, he will bear witness about me."

John 16:7-11, ". . . I tell you the truth: it is to your advantage that I go away, for if I do not go away, the Helper will not come to you. But if I go, I will send him to you. And when he comes, he will convict the world concerning sin and righteousness and judgment: concerning sin, because they do not believe in me; concerning righteousness, because I go to the Father, and you will see me no longer; concerning judgment, because the ruler of this world is judged."

John 16:13-14, "When the Spirit of truth comes, he will guide you into all the truth, for he will not speak on his own authority, but whatever he hears he will speak, and he will declare to you the things that are to come."

Acts 5:32, "And we are witnesses to these things, and so is the Holy Spirit, whom God has given to those who obey him."

Etc.

In truth, the omnipotent Holy Spirit with God the Father and Jesus' divinity created the Resurrection, Romans 1:4, 8:11, "If the Spirit of him who raised Jesus from the dead dwells in you, he who raised Christ Jesus from the dead will also give life to your mortal bodies through his Spirit who dwells in you." In and with the Resurrection, the miracle of miracles, the Spirit immortalized Jesus' humanity, now forever alive, guaranteeing believers the same in the life of the age to come.

On the Day of Pentecost, the Spirit proceeding from the Father and the Son entered the Church forever, choosing therefore the remnant Jesus had commanded to remain in Jerusalem, Acts 1:4. Then, on the fiftieth day after the Resurrection, he determined the Church's constitution for the new age. Acts 2:1-4,

> When the day of Pentecost arrived, [Jesus' followers] were all together in one place. And suddenly there came from heaven a sound like a mighty rushing wind, and it filled the entire house where they were sitting. And divided tongues as of fire appeared to them and rested on each one of them. And they were all filled with the Holy Spirit and began to speak in tongues as the Spirit gave them utterance.[81]

Not now the descent of the Spirit as a gentle dove; rather, in the name of the Father and of the Son, he entered the inchoate Church as a tempestuous wind and as a living flame, both impressively present to inspire Christian congregations for the duration of the second dispensation. Now, throughout the elongation of the new age, the energetic Spirit hurries the history of the world into the Eschaton, then eternally to complete the magnification of the Trinity in the powers of the new creation. Therefore, Matthew 24:1–44, Mark 13:1–37, and Luke 21:5–38 project watchfulness; such is the thrust too of Isaiah 65:17–25; Acts 3:17–26; 2 Peter 3:8–13; Revelation 21:1—22:5; etc.

Pentecost Day, circa AD 33, and the historic upsurge of the Church in Jerusalem calls for more intensive clarification.

Throughout the first dispensation, the Holy Spirit enlivened the created order, Genesis 1:2, breathed life into the Kingdom/Recreation, Genesis 3:14–19, primed the Christ for the Incarnation, Isaiah 61:1–4; and gathered the Old Testament documents into a unified body, a unity supported by the Septuagint. On the whole, however, he remained invisibly active, his workings alone visible to believers' observation; the Kingdom/Recreation lived as the obvious manifestation of his omnipotence, omniscience, and even omnipresence.

All through the second dispensation, and specifically after Pentecost Day, the Author at curating the New Testament documents moved a cumulative wave of authors into action. Between AD 55–65, Matthew, Mark, and Luke approximately 20–30 years after the Pentecost fact, wrote the Synoptics, Luke also the Book of the Acts. During the same decades, the Author/authors gave the Church Romans, 1&2 Corinthians, Galatians, Ephesians, Philippians, Colossians, 1&2 Thessalonians, 1&2 Timothy, Titus, Philemon, Hebrews, 1&2 Peter, and Jude. Before those men and witnesses perished, Luke 1:1–4; 1 Corinthians 15:3–11, the Author carried these authors along to record Jesus' reformation of the Kingdom/Recreation, its evidence the Church.

In the first century's late decades, the Spirit moved Apostle John, to write the Fourth Gospel, AD 85. In his Gospel, John decisively declared Jesus' prophetic word with respect to Pentecost Day. John 14:26, "... the Helper, the Holy Spirit,

---

81. This outpouring of the Spirit occurred again, Acts 4:31, 8:17, 10:44–48, 19:6, early manifestations among Gentiles to the entrance into the Faith.

whom the Father will send in my name, he will teach you all things and bring to your remembrance all that I have said to you." The last surviving apostle penned three letters, 1&2&3 John, AD 90, and The Revelation, AD 95–96.

Now, the living body of New Testament writings breathes out of powers of Acts 1:6–7, accelerating the Church, alive with Spirit of Jesus, actively to await the Christ on the clouds of heaven, indeed, "hastening the coming of the Day of God," 2 Peter 3:12.

With the omnipresent Spirit's regenerative powers, Jesus presents the inner and outer contours of the Kingdom/Recreation in the way of the Church; even while she walks through the valley of the shadow of death—rejecting hypocrites, ejecting unrepentant sinners, and liberating the imprisoned by sin—her members in the unity of hope seek the Eschaton.

All in all, to believe that the Trinity exists means to know God the Father, the indispensable foundation, God the Son, the expiatory Lord and Savior, and God the Spirit, the Life-giver. The Scriptures are replete to overflowing with their essential interworkings and with their revealed works of omnipotence, omniscience, and omnipresence in providence as well as grace. The Three, radiating majesty, act in unison with one will and goal, harmoniously, throughout the universe to magnify the Divinity by the creation of the Kingdom/Recreation, the Church, and the salvation of a people. And the fullness of salvation is through the Faith, believing and living the revelation of the Divinity.

This is to say, unequivocally, to believe God the Spirit's animation of the Kingdom/Recreation enlivens the trust in the Trinity's existence in every present.

In sum:

Now, in magnifying God the Father's groundwork for the Kingdom/Recreation, the Church believes the Faith eternally.

Now, in magnifying God the Son's reformation of the Kingdom/Recreation, the Church believes the Faith presently.

Now, in magnifying God the Spirit's animation of the Kingdom/Recreation, the Church believes the Faith ceaselessly.

Hence, the Divinity was, is, and will be glorified.

Third Summation

Upon this intense concentration on magnifying the Trinity—ascending out of depths of anti-trinitarian unfaithfulness onto the scriptural heights of glorying in the Divinity—the command to exult in him only intensifies. To gain that ultimate exaltation, Jesus breaks down all perfidious self-glorification, in the ruins of which to enable his people to strive for momentum in the Trinity's joy.

By patiently and reflectively reading Ephesians 1:3—2:10, know now how interwoven the revelation of the Trinity in Scriptures:

> Blessed be the God and Father of our Lord Jesus Christ, who has blessed us in Christ with every spiritual blessing in the heavenly places, even as he chose us in him before the foundation of the world, that we should be holy and blameless before him. In love he predestined us for adoption to himself as sons through Jesus Christ, according to the purpose of his will, to the praise of his glorious grace, with which he has blessed us in the Beloved. In him we have redemption through his blood, the forgiveness of our trespasses, according to the riches of his grace, which he lavished upon us, in all wisdom and insight making known to us the mystery of his will, according to his purpose, which he set forth in Christ as a plan[82] for the fullness of time, to unite all things in him, things in heaven and things on earth.

Scriptures reveal that God the Father—always and only in Christ Jesus—grounded predestination in the eternality's infinity prior to Day One.

> In him we have obtained an inheritance, having been predestined according to the purpose of him who works all things according to the counsel of his will, so that we who were the first to hope in Christ might be to the praise of his glory. In him you also, when you heard the word of truth, the gospel of your salvation, and believed in him, were sealed with the promised Holy Spirit, who is the guarantee of our inheritance until we acquire possession of it, to the praise of his glory.

Scriptures reveal that God the Son actuated predestination in the ongoing history of the Church.

> For this reason, because I have heard of your faith in the Lord Jesus and your love toward all the saints, I do not cease to give thanks for you, remembering you in my prayers, that the God of our Lord Jesus Christ, the Father of glory, may give you the Spirit of wisdom and of revelation in the knowledge of him, having the eyes of your hearts enlightened, that you may know what is the hope to which he has called you, what are the riches of his glorious inheritance in the saints, and what is the immeasurable greatness of his power toward us who believe, according to the

---

82. Revelation 5:8, with reference to the scroll that the ascended Jesus took from God the Father's right hand.

> working of his great might that he worked in Christ when he raised him from the dead and seated him at his right hand in the heavenly places, far above all rule and authority and power and dominion, and above every name that is named, not only in this age but also in the one to come. And he put all things under his feet and gave him as head over all things to the church, which is his body, the fullness of him who fills all in all.

Scriptures reveal that God the Spirit alive in the Church creates the Faith to believe all elements of redemption.

> And you were dead in the trespasses and sins in which you once walked, following the course of this world, following the prince of the power of the air, the spirit that is now at work in the sons of disobedience—among whom we all once lived in the passions of our flesh, carrying out the desires of the body and the mind, and were by nature children of wrath, like the rest of mankind. But God, being rich in mercy, because of the great love with which he loved us, even when we were dead in our trespasses, made us alive together with Christ—by grace you have been saved—and raised us up with him and seated us with him in the heavenly places in Christ Jesus, so that in the coming ages he might show the immeasurable riches of his grace in kindness toward us in Christ Jesus. For by grace you have been saved through faith. And this is not your own doing; it is the gift of God, not a result of works, so that no one may boast. For we are his workmanship, created in Christ Jesus for good works, which God prepared beforehand, that we should walk in them.

Because of the Divinity's inestimable grace, all citizens of the Kingdom/Recreation as the living members of the Church magnify God the Father, God the Son, and God the Spirit unceasingly, forever and a day.

Glorying in the Trinity recognizes the excellences of the Father, the Son, and the Spirit:

> God the Father, Jesus, and God the Spirit actuate believing the attribute of omnipotence, yet this omnipotence is one.

> God the Father, Jesus, and God the Spirit motivate believing the attribute of omniscience, yet this omniscience is one.

> God the Father, Jesus, and God the Spirit stimulate believing the attribute of omnipresence, yet this omnipresence is one.

> God the Father, Jesus, and God the Spirit express believing the attribute of willpower, yet this willpower is one.

In a similar manner, Jesus' divinity and humanity each exercise willpower, yet because of his humanity's sinlessness the two wills work in perfect concert.

This meta-teaching grounds and upholds all biblical doctrine, the whole constitutively one work.

Appendix One-Two

ANCIENT CORRUPTIONS

Scriptures manifest the transcendent and immanent Divinity gloriously omnipotent, omniscient, and omnipresent. Transcendent, he displays incommunicable attributes to magnify his trinitarian glories. Immanent, he infuses his communicable excellences into people, that they too glorify him. Omnipotent, he compels all creation to serve his magnification. Omniscient, he comprehends the entirety of the created order and wills all creation to know as well as worship him. Omnipresent, he draws the universe in its wholeness to acknowledge him, Romans 1:19-20. The Scriptures exude the glories of the Trinity.

Nevertheless, the Trinity proscribes rational and also mystical penetration into his transcendent attributes, thereby to gain access to his being. He is not a logical and comprehensible thing. One attempt at rationally explaining the unexplainable? AD 185/6-232/3 Origen's Neoplatonic Bible interpretation conformed the Word of God to the then current Greek mythological paradigm and gained a dominance euphemistically fastened down as the Great Tradition.[1]

---

1. Barrett. *Simply Trinity*, 35.
Olson and Hall. *Guides to Theology: The Trinity*, 74.

1

Before dismissing the Great Tradition, first a concise *portrayal* of the Trinity—risking even minimal transgression of the Second Commandment. Eternally, the Three-in-One animates his many excellences for magnifying the One-in-Three. Without a trace of subordination, God the Father glorifies God the Son and God the Spirit, God the Son glorifies God the Spirit and God the Father, and God the Spirit glorifies God the Father and God the Son:[2] the Three are one in being and one in willing. What is true of one is true of the others. From eternity to eternity, in this eternal unity of glory, the Divinity is incomprehensible.

Prior to the Adamic Fall, the Trinity ranged freely inside and outside the created order, all attributes unhindered and unlimited in magnificence. Upon the Fall, the Trinity in unity willed and generated the Kingdom/Recreation, therein displaying anew all trinitarian splendors. Now, the Church consciously and openly confesses the Trinity and his attributes; by acknowledging all trinitarian magnificence, she, at reading the Scriptures, bows humbly and fearfully at categorizing the Divinity's excellences.

God the Father's Attributes

(without complete accreditation)

The Father is unassailable in transcendent exaltations:

> Aseity (= absolute self-sufficiency, independence, and autonomy of divinity), omnipotence,[3] omniscience, omnipresence, supremacy, immutability, eternity, intangibility, immortality, unchangeability,[4] and invisibility.

> In his transcendence, the Father is unsearchable in eminence.

> At the same time, with absolute freedom, the Father imparts immanent attributes:

> mercy, faithfulness, truth,[5] love, grace, goodness, trust, longsuffering, sovereignty, righteousness, wisdom, freedom, willpower, and holiness.[6]

---

2. Toon and Spiceland. *One God in Trinity*, 2, "These three are fully equal in every divine perfection. They posses alike the fullness of the divine essence."

3. First Peter 1:5; etc.

4. James 1:17; etc.

5. John 7:28; etc.

6. Revelation 15:4; etc.

With all exaltations, God the Father out of the trinitarian communion prepared the groundwork for the first creation and then the Kingdom/Recreation. In the bountiful strength of these excellences, the Church moves eschatologically onwards.

God the Son's Attributes

(without complete accreditation)

The Son is unassailable in transcendent attributes:

> aseity (= absolute self-sufficiency, independence, and autonomy of divinity), omnipotence,[7] omniscience,[8] omnipresence,[9] supremacy, immutability,[10] eternity,[11] intangibility, immortality, unchangeability,[12] and invisibility.

In his transcendence, the Son is unsearchable in eminence.

At the same time, God the Son with absolute freedom imparts his immanent glories:

> mercy, faithfulness, truth,[13] love, grace, goodness, trust, longsuffering, sovereignty,[14] righteousness,[15] wisdom,[16] freedom, willpower, and holiness.[17]

With all exaltation, God the Son out of the trinitarian communion commanded the original creation to come forth into his presence and now with the same command performance draws the Kingdom/Recreation into his presence.

   7. Psalm 139:13; Jeremiah 23:24; Matthew 18:20, 28, 18, 20, 28:18; Luke 8:25; Colossians 1:16; 1 Peter 1:5; Jude 3; etc.
   8. Psalm 139:3; Matthew 18:20, 28:20; John 2:25, 1:47-49, 16:30, 21:17; Romans 11:33; etc.
   9. Psalm 139:8; Jeremiah 23:24; Matthew 9:4; Romans 11:33; Ephesians 4:10; Colossians 2:3, 3:11; 1 Peter 3:22; etc.
   10. Hebrews 1:10-12/Psalm 102:25-27; Hebrews 13:8; etc.
   11. Micah 5:2; John 1:2; Revelation 1:8, 17; Psalm 90:2; etc.
   12. Malachi 3:6; etc.
   13. John 14:6; Revelation 3:7; etc.
   14. John 5:27; 1 Corinthians 3:10-15; 2 Corinthians 5:10-13; Philippians 2:9-10; 1 Peter 3:22; Revelation 19:16, 20:11-15; etc.
   15. Acts 3:14; etc.
   16. Matthew 12:42; Luke 11:49; 1 Corinthians 1:24; etc.
   17. Revelation 15:4; Acts 3:14; etc.
   Argyle. *Knowing Christianity: God in the New Testament*, 17, "God is not only Himself holy; He is the sole source of all holiness in places or people or whatever is holy."

At the point of the Incarnation, the bonding of God the Son's divinity with humanity in Jesus, the Trinity created a hierarchy, the Son's humanity forever subordinate to his divinity, to God the Father, and to God the Spirit. Such distinguishes divinity and humanity. In terms of divinity, Jesus is the equal of God the Father and God the Spirit. In terms of his humanity, he is subordinate, serving.

God the Spirit's Attributes

(without complete accreditation)

God the Spirit is unassailable in transcendent exaltations:

> aseity (= absolute self-sufficiency, independence, and autonomy of divinity), omnipotence,[18] omniscience,[19] omnipresence,[20] supremacy, immutability, eternity,[21] intangibility, immortality, unchangeability,[22] and invisibility.

In his transcendence, the Spirit is unsearchable in eminence.

At the same time, the Spirit with absolute freedom imparts his immanent attributes:

> mercy, faithfulness, truth,[23] love, grace, goodness, trust, longsuffering, sovereignty, righteousness,[24] wisdom,[25] freedom, willpower,[26] and holiness.[27]

With all excellences, God the Spirit out of the trinitarian communion breathed life into the original creation and now pours life into the Kingdom/Recreation.

The Trinity elected to call forth the universe, subsequently the Kingdom/Recreation. The Kingdom initially encapsulated the innumerable galaxies—the entirety of totality. Within the space/time boundaries of the

18. Romans 15:19; etc.
19. First Corinthians 2:10; etc.
20. Psalm 139:7; etc.
21. Hebrews 9:14; etc.
22. Malachi 3:6; etc.
23. John 14:17; 1 John 5:6; etc.
24. Acts 3:14; etc.
25. First Corinthians 2:6–16; etc.
26. Barrett. *Simply Trinity,* 56, "Will and power are not separate from the essence, as if they can be divided up in different degrees among the persons, for example. No, will and power are to be identified with the one essence."
27. John 16:7–14; etc.

created order, upon Adam's Fall, the Divinity commenced upon the reformation of the Kingdom, and therein the beauties of the Recreation.

2

Christ Jesus created the New Church at a time and in a world fermenting in Greek mythology/philosophy, Plato's Platonism and Plotinus' Neo-Platonism. During the initial centuries of the second dispensation, the Lord and Savior raised Christian thinkers still blind to the religious environment, primarily men who understood and hence interpreted the Scriptures' Trinity according to the then current mythological/philosophical paradigm, a frame of mind dominated by ontological issues of origins. Those theologians continued by default in that culture's way of reasoning to sort out matters of historical foundation, the engrossing entanglement of the day. Locked into that mythological/philosophical temperament, they, with Greek language patterns and rational thought systems, reduced the revelation of the Trinity to fit the disposition of the day.

Toiling with pagan ideas to know the Divinity's origin, Plotinus,[28] d. AD 270, by way of Platonic formatting, invented a "perfect" First Principle, the One, a god consisting of pure light, totally immaterial, that had originated the universe. This One through thinking, mentation, emanated a series of spiritual worlds strung together in a (long) line. The further away those immaterial worlds extended from the First Principle, the less spiritual and the more material, or evil, these became. That evil materiality imprisoned particles of light, human souls, which had to discover a way up through the emanations to the pure light of the One, all the while motivated by a demiurge, a sort of paganized Christ figure.

Origen[29] adapted this Neo-Platonist idolatry for emerging trinitarian interpretation and formulated a monist[30] interpretation of origins. His was one of many similar ways to understand the foundation of the universe. Origen then identified the Neo-Platonist One with the absolutely eternal God the Father. To account for the universe and this materially evil world,

---

28. Holmes. *The Quest for the Trinity*, 64.

29. Holmes. *The Quest for the Trinity*, 37, ". . . Origen of Alexandria (c. 185–254) is perhaps the first Christian writer both to reflect self-consciously on how to interpret the Scriptures, and to put his ideas into practice in the disciplined production of commentaries."

30. Toon and Spiceland. *One God in Trinity*, 50, ". . . the first and fundamental concern of all the patristic writers was to preserve a pure monotheism. In the second century in particular this was closely linked to the idea that God was the creator of the universe and Father of all mankind."

he imagined that God the Father, too pure to emanate evil, by eternal generation,[31] filiation, created from his own substance another God, God the Son,[32] the subordinate agent for originating the universe and accountable for evil. As also the savior of the light particles imprisoned in material evil, the Demiurge had to motivate human souls to journey up the emanations into the Light. This filiation by eternal generation Origen invoked as an analogical incarnation, an unhistorical event.[33] As a Greek mythologist/philosopher, Origen's concentration of interest lay in (oxymoronic) trinitarian ontology, the ancient Greek theory of origins, and not in the first historical Kingdom, not in the Kingdom/Recreation, and definitely not in the Incarnation dominant in the Christian Scriptures.

Because God the Son's filiation[34] occurred in the Father's eternality, God the Son was eternal too, yet subordinate to the Father. By positioning the primary Incarnation as filiation, Origen locked God the Father and God the Son into an eternal hierarchy.[35] Since Origen's Father-God existed immeasurably far beyond any involvement with evil, he had God the Son accountable for the universe and responsible for the salvation of human souls.[36]

31. Holmes. *The Quest for the Trinity*, 76, "Origen's images of the generation of the Son are dynamic, rather than static: this is something that is always happening (if such language has any purchase on eternity)."
Norris. *Sources of Early Christian Thought: The Christological Controversy*, 14, "The two substances continue unaltered in the one person and provide the bases for two kinds of activity, human and divine."

32. Gunton, Colin, "And in One Lord, Jesus Christ . . . Begotten, Not Made," 35–48, in Seitz. *Nicene Christianity*, 35, ". . . the Son, the second person of the Trinity, has an origin that is in some way posterior to that of God the Father."
Barrett. *Simply Trinity*, 171, ". . . the Son cannot be less than his source (the Father), because there is no hierarchy in the Trinity. The Father is not greater than the Son—not in any way."
Norris. *Sources of Early Christian Thought: The Christological Controversy*, 15, "Origen believed, as against his predecessors, that God begot his Wisdom or Logos eternally—that there never was a time when the Logos did not exist."

33. Toon and Spiceland. *One God in Trinity*, 55, "Origen understood quite clearly that the central issue for trinitarianism was the question of the internal relations of the persons of the Godhead, which by the very nature of God, must be eternal. The Incarnation could only be the enactment in time of a generation which lay beyond the temporal—ergo, the Son, had been generated in and from eternity."

34. Gunton, Colin, "And in One Lord, Jesus Christ . . . Begotten, Not Made," 35–48, in Seitz. *Nicene Christianity*, 37–38, "To say that Jesus Christ is begotten is to use a metaphor, for clearly, whatever else is the case with his being begotten in time in the womb of Mary, he is not there eternally begotten."

35. Toon and Spiceland. *One God in Trinity*, 55, "It followed . . . that submission as a basic ingredient of his divine personhood—hence the Son was eternally subordinate to the Father."

36. Gunton, Colin, "And in One Lord, Jesus Christ . . . Begotten, Not Made," 35–48, in Seitz. *Nicene Christianity*, 42, "Athanasius believes that Jesus Christ is the mediator

To account for the Holy Spirit, Origen, following Plotinus' Neo-Platonist imagination, spirated him from God the Father and God the Son; by this eternal proceeding from the Father and the Son, Origen accounted for the Spirit, placing him third in the hierarchical structure—the eternal Father more than the eternal Son and the eternal Son more than the eternal Spirit.

When Arius,[37] AD 256–336, denied Jesus' divinity,[38] the Church's theological leaders assumed Origen's mythical filiation and spiration, which solution then existed outside Arius' tampering with Christological interpretation. With God the Father eternally begetting God the Son, which eternalized the Son, there was never a *time* when the Son was not; his filiation too existed from eternity to eternity.

At establishing a mythological/philosophical origin for all existence, early theological thinkers, Origenists, diverted attention from magnifying the Trinity to eternal relations of origin,[39] which was the Devil's intention. For where in Scriptures is such concentration on trinitarian ontology?

Origenist trinitarian eisegesis developed in complexity until approximately the sixteenth century AD, seeking sympathetic understanding; all the while, its devotees grew a unbiblical grammar and philosophical terminology in order 1) to speculate about this ontology and 2) to bar believers from confessing the Trinity's magnificence, two devilish aims. The lexicon? *Ousia, homousios,*[40] *homoiousios, prosopon, persona,* hypostasis, hypostaseis, subsistence, hypostatic union, consubsistence, essence, filiation, eternal generation,

---

of creation returning to his creation to restore the created order to its maker and so enables it to fulfill its original purpose."

37. Gunton, Colin, "And in One Lord, Jesus Christ . . . Begotten, Not Made," 35–48, in Seitz. *Nicene Christianity,* 35, "Certain heresies are archetypal as attractive solutions to difficulties that are intrinsic to the faith and will therefore continue to appear in every generation."

38. Torrance, Alan, "Being of One Substance with the Father," 49–61, in Seitz. *Nicene Christianity,* 53, "For Arius, . . . the Son was not God but belonged to the contingent, creaturely realm. The Son was a creature, albeit the first creature (*proton ktisma*)."

Holmes. *The Quest For the Trinity,* 86, "The point of departure seems to have been Alexander's echoing of Origen's teaching on eternal generation: the Father can never be without the Son, or he would not be Father."

39. Barrrett. *Simply Trinity,* 25, "The word 'origin' is fitting because we are describing where these three persons come from (e.g., the Son is *from* the Father). The word 'eternal' is appropriate since this is God we have in view. And the word 'relation' is another way of referring to the *persons* of the Trinity, specifically what is so unique about each of them (e.g., the Father is unbegotten, the Son is begotten, and the Spirit is spirated)."

40. Torrance, Alan, "Being of One Substance with the Father,' 49–61, in Seitz. *Nicene Christianity,* 49, "The intention is clear—to affirm with unambiguous clarity that the One whom we meet in the person of Jesus is none other than God—God came not merely *in* a human being but *as human.*"

spiration, eternal proceeding, one substance/three persons, the Person of God the Father, the Person of God the Son, the Person of God the Spirit, subordination, relations of origin, *heteroousios*, modes of subsistence; etc. This extra-biblical language and way of speaking became necessary only in order to navigate the dark currents and darker undercurrents of the Great Tradition.

The familiar person-talk of the Great Tradition means to identify and personalize the Three-of-the-Trinity, which 1) locks each of the Divinity into constantly changing definitions of personhood,[41] and 2) compels each of the Three into humanly comprehensible divinities.[42] Both start idolizing.

---

41. Personhood consists in struggles for phenomena as community, independence, and passions of love. To fit the Trinity's Three into forms of personhood only diminishes each one into idols.

Olson and Hall. *Guides to Theology: The Trinity*, 36, "Although God's being is characterized by the hypostatic distinctions of Father, Son, and Spirit, all three persons are one in their will and activity. They are not autonomous persons in the modern nuance of 'individual,' each with its own separate 'ego' and 'center' of consciousness." 98–99, "(Karl) Rahner was concerned that the concept 'person' may not be the one best suited to express faithfully the distinctions within the trinitarian life of God. In *The Trinity* he argued that use of 'person' following medieval philosopher Boethius' definition of individual substance of a rational nature' inevitably misleads people to think of the Trinity as 'three individuals.' According to Rahner (closely following at least one strand of Augustine's trinitarian thought), there are not three consciousnesses [in God]; rather, one consciousness subsists in a threefold way. There is only one real consciousness in God, which is shared by Father, Son, and Spirit, by each in his own proper way.' Rahner was concerned to avoid what he saw the inevitable implication of importing a modern, Enlightenment view of 'person' as 'subject' into the threefoldness of the Trinity."

Holmes. *The Quest for the Trinity*, 8, "Decisively, however, in the nineteenth century the concept of 'person' became explicitly and inseparably identified with 'personality', rendering it unusable in theological discourse."

Barrett. *Simply Trinity*, 86, "Persons are redefined according to their relationships: focus on mutuality, societal interaction."

White. *The Forgotten Trinity*, 24, "... we must not succumb to the temptation to read the term 'person' as if we are talking about finite, self-contained human beings. What 'person' means when we speak of the Trinity is quite different than when we speak of creatures such as ourselves,"

42. How then to name the Three-of-the-Trinity biblically, if not addressing each as a person:

The name God the Father spontaneously brings to mind his contextual groundwork in the original creation, the Exodus, and the Incarnation. Out of the historical-redemptive way of the Scriptures, he originates.

The name Jesus freely calls forth his bonding in divinity and humanity.

The name the Son of God remembers concretely Jesus' salvific workings from the Incarnation through to the Eschaton.

The name the Son of Man activates concentration on Jesus' judgeship in the first and great Judgment as well as the second and final Judgment.

Jesus' multiple Old Testament and New identifications stress his historical-redemptive workings for raising the Church to glorify the Trinity.

The name God the Spirit easily deliberates on his animating presence throughout the Church.

As Origen's Neo-Platonism *resolved* pagan questions of trinitarian ontology, the Great-Tradition theologians then adopted and adapted Origen's eisegetical discounting of the glory of the Trinity. Because his was the more developed or the better known, this version of the spirit of Greek mythology compelled the people of the Faith to evade, contrary to the Scriptures, the Trinity's glories and glorification.

When Arian speculation[43] denied God the Son's divinity and held him up as a unique human being, an immense theological struggle broke open to know and confess the Scriptures' basic doctrine, the trinitarian. For Jesus' humanity *and* divinity drove the Religion's heartbeat: without his divinity the trinitarian teaching crumbled into dust. Therefore, in the fourth-century AD, trinitarian-motivated debates and councils strove for and against Jesus' divinity. Under Caesars' aegis, two major councils, the Nicaean, AD 325, and the Constantinopolitan, AD 381, dominated church life. At that time, Origen's ontology, which *acknowledged* the Son's divinity, as well as the Spirit's, informed the Church's understanding of the Trinity, while denying Arius' heresy/apostasy; the orthodox bishops in council and in debate refused the ruin of salvation. Thinkers as Athanasius, AD 293–373, grasped Origen's trinitarian hierarchy to interpret the Bible to oppose Arianism's anti-trinitarian onslaughts. Augustine,[44]

Reading and interpreting the Bible with the mind of Christ and through the indwelling Spirit requires nothing of the Great Tradition. By naming each of the Trinity along with masculine pronouns follows the biblical pattern.

43. Barrett. *Simply Trinity*, 35, "... the most dangerous heretics knew how to quote the Bible better than anyone, so it was essential to use extrabiblical words to safeguard the Bible's Trinity from manipulation."

Olson and Hall. *Guides to Theology: the Trinity*, 32, "The Word could not belong to the Father's substance. Instead, Arius argued that the Son was an exalted creature, elevated above all others, but still a creation of God."

Norris. *Sources of Early Christian Thought: The Christological Controversy*, 17, "Logically enough, therefore, his doctrine of the Logos was so formulated as to express two convictions: first, that the Logos cannot be God in the proper sense; second, that the Logos performs an essential mediatorial role in the relation of God to world."

Rush. *Sources of Early Christian Thought: The Trinitarian Controversy*, 32, "Nor does he have being with the Father, as certain individuals mention things relatively and bring into the discussion two unbegotten causes."

Anatolios. *Retrieving Nicaea*, 17, "The fluidity of this model of divinity allowed Arius to balance scriptural attributions of divine honor to the Son with a strict interpretation of biblical monotheism."

Rush. *Sources of Early Christian Thought: The Trinitarian Controversy*, 35, Arius: "He who before was not, later came into existence; and when he came into existence, he became as every human being is by nature."

44. Augustine. *Nicene and Post-Nicene Fathers*, III, 20, "... therefore that they are not three Gods, but one God: although the Father hath begotten the Son, and so He who is the Father is not the Son; and so the Son is begotten by the Father, and so the

AD 354–430, and John Calvin,[45] AD 1509–1564, also superimposed this heresy/apostasy on the Trinity, hurting thereby the magnification of the Divinity. After Calvin, interest in the Great Tradition failed; its perpetuation continued unenthusiastically. The monstrously hungry secularization of the Renaissance-Enlightenment[46]-Modernist spirit over pivotal centuries had the Church struggle for survival.[47]

3

Origen's erroneous trinitarian theology became firmly lodged in the Church's universal creeds, pagan heterodoxies ensconced in the Nicaean and the Athanasian. Below, the italicized sections expose the faults.

The Nicene Creed

> We believe in one God, the Father Almighty,
> Maker of heaven and earth,
> of all things visible and invisible.
> And in one Lord, Jesus Christ, the only-begotten Son of God,
> *begotten of the Father before all ages;*[48]
> *God of God, Light of Light, true God of true God;*
> *begotten, not made,*
> *of one substance with the Father;*
> through whom all things were made.[49]
> Who, for us men and our salvation,

Son is not the Father; and the Holy Spirit is neither the Father nor the Son, but only the Spirit of the Father and of the Son, Himself also co-equal with the Father and the Son, and pertaining to the unity of the Trinity."

45. Calvin. *Institutes*, I.13.18, "... the observance of an order is not meaningless or superfluous, when the Father is thought of as first, then from him the Son, and finally from both the Spirit."

46. Braaten, Carl E, "The Reality of the Resurrection," 107–18, in Seitz. *Nicene Christianity*, 108, "The motto of the Enlightenment was '*saperse aude!*'—have courage to use you own reason."

47. Rahner. *The Trinity*, 10–11, "... despite their orthodox confession of the Trinity, Christians are, in their practical life, almost mere 'monotheists.' We must be willing to admit that, should the doctrine of the Trinity have to be dropped as false, the major part of the religious literature could well remain virtually unchanged."

48. This is the first of two estranged incarnational mentions in the Nicene; the other points to the virgin Mary.

49. God the Son was involved in the work of creation with God the Father, 1 Corinthians 8:6.

came down from heaven and became incarnate by the Holy
Spirit of the virgin Mary,
and was made man.
He was crucified for us under Pontius Pilate;
he suffered and was buried;
and the third day he arose, according to the Scriptures,
and ascended into heaven, and sits at the right of the Father,
and he will come again with glory to judge the living and the dead;
whose kingdom shall have no end.
And we believe in the Holy Spirit, the Lord and Giver of life,
who proceeds from the Father and the Son;
who with the Father and the Son[50] is worshipped and glorified;
who spoke through the prophets.[51]
And we believe one holy catholic and apostolic church.
We acknowledge one baptism for the forgiveness of sins;
and we look forward to the resurrection of the dead,
and the life of the world to come.
Amen.

The Athanasian Creed

Whoever desires to be saved must above all things hold to the catholic faith.
Unless a man keeps it in its entirety inviolate, he will assuredly perish eternally.

Now this is the catholic faith, that we worship one God in trinity and trinity in unity, without either confusing the *persons*, or dividing the substance.
For the Father's *person* is one, the Son's another, the Holy Spirit's another;

---

50. Smail, "The Holy Spirit in the Holy Trinity," 149–65, in Seitz. *Nicene Christianity*, 107, "Attention is so concentrated on the binitarian question of the right relationship of the Father to the Son that the properly trinitarian question that deals with the relating of the Spirit to both Father and Son is dealt with in a way that lacks focus and specificity and that, on any reckoning, is quite inadequate to the rich biblical and especial New Testament material that deals with the pre- and post-Pentecost activity of the Spirit among God's people."

51. Rusch. *Sources of Early Christian Thought: The Trinitarian Controversy*, 4, "A special debt was owed to the Jewish philosopher Philo of Alexandria, who taught that the divine Logos had spoken through the prophets and had been the subject of the theophanies of the Old Testament."

but the Godhead of the Father, the Son, and the Holy Spirit is one,
their glory is equal, their majesty is co-eternal.

Such as the Father is, such is the Son, such is also the Holy Spirit.
The Father is uncreate, the Son uncreate, the Holy Spirit uncreate.
The Father is infinite, the Son infinite, the Holy Spirit infinite.
The Father is eternal, the Son eternal, the Holy Spirit eternal.
Yet there are not three eternals, but one eternal; just as there
not three uncreates or three infinites, but one uncreate and one
infinite.
In the same way the Father is almighty, the Son almighty, the
Holy Spirit almighty; yet there are not three almighties, but one
almighty.

Thus the Father is God, the Son God, the Holy Spirit God; and
yet there are not three Gods, but there is one God.
Thus the Father is Lord, the Son Lord, the Holy Spirit Lord;
and yet there are not three Lords, but there is one Lord.
Because just as we are compelled by Christian truth to acknowledge each *person* separately to be both God and Lord,
so we are forbidden by the catholic religion to speak of three
Gods or Lords.

The Father is from none, not made nor created nor begotten
The Son is from the Father alone, not made nor created but begotten.[52]
The Holy Spirit is from the Father and the Son,
not made nor created nor begotten but proceeding.
So there is one Father, not three Fathers; one Son, not three
Sons; one Holy Spirit, not three Holy Spirits.
And in this trinity there is nothing before or after, nothing
greater or less, but all three *persons* are co-eternal with each
other and co-equal.
Thus in all things, as has been stated above, both trinity in
unity and unity in trinity must be worshipped.
So he who desires to be saved should think thus of the Trinity.

It is necessary, however, to eternal salvation that he should also
believe in the incarnation of our Lord Jesus Christ.
Now the right faith is that we should believe and confess that our
Lord Jesus Christ, the Son of God, is equally both God and man.

---

52. This is the first of two estranged incarnational mentions in the Athanasian; the other points to the virgin Mary.

He is God from the Father's substance, begotten before time; and
he is man from his mother's substance, born in time.
Perfect God, perfect man composed of a human soul and human flesh, equal to the Father in respect of his divinity,
less than the Father in respect to his humanity.

Who, although he is God and man, is nevertheless not two, but one Christ.
He is one, however, not by the transformation of his divinity into flesh,
but by taking up of his humanity into God; one certainly not by confusion of substance,
but by oneness of *person*.
For just as soul and flesh are one man, so God and man are one Christ.
Who suffered for our salvation, descended into hell, rose from the dead, ascended to heaven, sat down at the Father's right hand, from where he will come to judge the living and the dead; at whose coming all men will rise again with their bodies, and will render an account of their deeds; and those who have done good will go to eternal life, those who have done evil to eternal fire.

This is the catholic faith.
Unless a man believes it faithfully and steadfastly,
he cannot be saved.
Amen.

Every congregational recitation of, every meditative reflection on, and every studious working through these universal statements of faith consents to deflate the magnification of the Trinity and then harden the Church in heresy, if not apostasy.

Appendix Two-Two

CONTEMPORARY CORRUPTIONS

SINCE THE RISING OF the Renaissance-Enlightenment and evolution into its 20th-century Modernist force of progressivism, this rationalistic piety with spellbinding fixation in several ways debased trinitarian teaching. Three-in-One? One-in-Three? Such anomaly mocks mathematical rules of engagement. Instead, unfaithful thinkers sundered the basic biblical doctrine from its source to revel in the enlightened spirit of Modernism-Postmodernism and reinterpret trinitarian teaching, making the Trinity conform to human vagaries of imagination.

1

Alongside the Great Tradition, two continuously cycling misconceptions of the past linger, rationalistically appealing tritheism and modalism; both are attempts at colonizing monotheism in the Church.

Tritheism[53] separates the Three-of-the-Trinity into distinctive deities eternally committed to work in unity. By forcing the Trinity into an

---

53. Rhodes. *Christ Before the Manger*, 23, ". . . the belief that there are three Gods rather than three persons within the Godhead."

Nicole, Roger, "The Meaning of the Trinity," 1–9, in Olson and Hall. *Guides to Theology: The Trinity*, 3, "*Tritheism* . . . asserts the eternal existence of the three and their full equality but it denies the monotheistic doctrine of the uniqueness of God."

eisegetically alluring pantheon runs contrary to the trinitarian rule of faith,[54] the recognition of the unity and multiplicity of the Divinity. Moreover, for every pantheon, its human handlers demand that one god dominate—in the Canaanite, Baal; in the Assyrian, Asher; in the Babylonian, Marduk, and in the Greek/Roman, Zeus/Jupiter. In tritheism, God the Father became the chief deity. In each pantheon, human handlers push and shove a god more authoritative than others into a henotheistic system. Tritheistic and henotheistic idolatries, idolatrous impieties, elude magnifying the Trinity.

Modalism,[55] or Sabellianism,[56] or Patripassianism deludes in distinctive ways:

One. Monarchial modalism finds that one God exists: the dominant God the Father changes into God the Son, who then changes into God the Spirit; in each modalistic form, God the Father takes over and infers that he, a god beyond all gods in the Origenistic way came to suffer the Crucifixion. This major discrepancy with respect to the Scriptures nullifies its relevance as well as longevity. Monarchialism rises and dies.

Two. Dynamic modalism[57] supposes that God the Father fluidly morphs into God the Son and then transmutes into God the Spirit, in the process even as Monarchialism, it bypasses the Incarnation and hence the reality of the Kingdom/Recreation. All attention falls on the progression from the one into the other to maintain monotheism and escape from magnifying the Trinity.

In short, tritheism and modalism by sustaining monotheism subtract from magnifying the Trinity, forcing the Divinity into an idolic mold.

---

54. Holmes. *The Quest For the Trinity,* 75, "The rule of faith is triadic . . . and so the theological question of the Trinity is not whether to worship Father, Son, and Holy Spirit, but how to understand the triune life of God."

55. Rhodes. *Christ Before the Manger,* 23, ". . . we must not conclude that the Godhead is *one person only* and that the triune aspect of his being is no more than three fields of interest, activities, or modes of manifestation."

Nicole, Roger, "The Meaning of the Trinity," 1–9, in Toon and Spiceland. *One God in Trinity,* 2, "It denies that God *eternally* exists in three persons. Rather it views the three as successive manifestations of one and the same person: God variously presented as Father or as Son or as Holy Spirit."

56. Barrett. *Simply Trinity,* 145, "According to Sabellianism (also called modalistic monarchianism), God is not three persons but one person who merely changes into three different forms."

Rush. *Early Sources of Christian Thought: The Trinitarian Controversy,* 9, "Sabellianism taught that God was a monad, expressing itself in three operations."

57. Rhodes. *Christ Before the Manger,* 20, ". . . Oneness Pentecostals, who deny the triune nature of God and say that the Father, Son, and Holy Spirit are three 'manifestations' (*not* persons) of the one God."

To these three, the Great Tradition, tritheism, and modalism, thinkers bound by the Modernist spirit of the 20th century added other deformations of the Trinity.

2

Thinkers in 20th-century Modernism, reactionary, stirred interest in trinitarian theology in line with the Renaissance-Enlightenment spirit; basically a Eurocentric movement, without little recourse to the Scriptures, these theologians from out of respective systems of thought broached distinctive ideas[58] that fail to glorify the Trinity and build up the Faith according to the basic biblical doctrine.

These eisegetical attempts at rationalistic piety—seeming conformity to the Scriptures—forced into the public square spurious sorts of trinitarian relevance. This rationalism tampered with unity in being and unity in will, to draw the Trinity onto a understandable human level. Of these attempts at trinitarian significance:

Karl Barth, AD 1886–1968, for relevancy found it necessary to eliminate Jesus' divinity by exclusively focusing on God the Father, ". . . He is who He reveals Himself as being, namely, the Father[59] of Jesus Christ His Son, who as such is Himself God. He can be so, because He is Himself the Father in Himself, because Fatherhood is an eternal mode of existence of the divine essence. In Him whose name, kingdom, and will Jesus reveals, in His actual individual distinction from this His revealer, though also in His individual communion with him, we have to do with God Himself."[60] With this realignment of the Trinity, Barth moved on. "From this unity of the content of the revelation with the Person of the Revealer we therefore inferred the original and peculiar meaning of the Fatherhood of God, that He

---

58. Barrett. *Simply Trinity*, 74, ". . . they needed a Trinity radically different from the historic, orthodox model; they needed a *social* Trinity that matched their vision for society."

59. This Fatherhood the Author/authors of the Scriptures revealed first in the New Testament. Hence, Barth's naming carries an Origenistic weight.

60. Barth. *The Doctrine of the Word of God*, 1/1, 448.
Jenson, "For Us . . . He Was Made Man," 75–85, in Seitz. *Nicene Christianity*, 76, ". . . Karl Barth, who taught that saving us belongs to the purpose for which God creates us, not in a systematic way or by any sort of implication, but just as an *historical* coherence within God's act of decision."
Pannenberg. *Systematic Theology*, I, 296, "Barth could thus think of the doctrine of the Trinity as an exposition of the subjectivity of God in his revelation. This being so, there is no room for a plurality of persons in the one God but only for different modes of being in the one divine subjectivity."

is the Father, because He is the Father of the only-begotten Son."[61] By declaring Jesus of Nazareth God without divine provenance, Barth purportedly brought the Trinity closer to the people of the Church, to generate interest.[62]

Karl Rahner, 1904–1984 AD, to entwine life into the trinitarian doctrine, developed a rule: *"The 'economic' Trinity is the 'immanent' Trinity and the 'immanent' Trinity is the 'economic' Trinity."*[63] This tenet, making

---

61. Barth. The *Doctrine of the Word of God*, 1/1, 471.

Holmes. *The Quest for the Trinity*, 6, "Where Barth did perhaps depart more decisively from the Reformation inheritance is his denial of any existence of the Second Person of the Trinity, the divine Son, that is not also the existence of Jesus Christ, the man from Nazareth."

Weber. *Karl Barth's Church Dogmatics*, 41, "Now according to the New Testament witness the 'simple and unique reality, Jesus Christ,' is to be defined in this way: 'The Word or Son of God became a man, and was called Jesus of Nazareth; therefore this man, Jesus of Nazareth, was God's Word or God's Son' . . . Or: 'God's Son means Jesus of Nazareth; Jesus of Nazareth is God's Son . . . .'"

Olson and Hall. *The Trinity*, 97, "In his doctrine of reconciliation (especially in CD IV/1) Barth brought the immanent and economic Trinities together by positing that the Son's journey is God's own journey and that the Son's self-humiliation in birth, life, and death is an expression of God's transcendence. God is exalted in the humility of the Son."

62. Tillich. *Systematic Theology*, III, 285. "It was a mistake of Barth to start his Prolegomena with what, so to speak, are the Prolegomena, the doctrine of the Trinity. It could be said that in his system this doctrine falls from heaven, the heaven of an unmediated biblical and ecclesiastical authority."

Anatolios. *Retrieving Nicaea*, 5, "Thus Karl Barth . . . sought to reassert the ontological identity between the eternal Word and the incarnate Word, to the point of affirming that the eternal word is in some sense eternally incarnate, or at least *incarnandus*."

63. Rahner. *The Trinity*, 22.

Olson and Hall. *The Trinity*, 98, "This has been dubbed 'Rahner's Rule' by contemporary theologians. Rahner was concerned that too much focus on the inner life of God and especially on God's unity of being ('simplicity') led the church into a neglect of the Trinity and of the intrinsic link between it and the doctrine of salvation. He wanted to make the Trinity more practical by demonstrating its connection with salvation. His goal was to forbid or discourage all speculation about the immanent Trinity that was not relevant to salvation (including Christian life). He was convinced that the only purpose of speaking about God's immanent triune being is to guard against dissolving God into history and to protect God's transcendence and the graciousness of salvation. The immanent Trinity, however, must be regarded as the 'background,' so to speak, of the economic Trinity, and the economic Trinity must be regarded as the outworking of the immanent Trinity. Whatever is true of the triune being of God in the economy of salvation must be seen as true of God-in-himself, and whatever is true of God-in-himself must be seen as affected by (not constituted by) the incarnation and sending of the Spirit."

Barrett. *Simply Trinity*, 77, "In some sense, Rahner equates the immanent and the economic, so that the two are one and the same."

Holmes. *The Quest For the Trinity*, 10, ". . . the doctrine of the Trinity has become detached from salvation history. Rahner's proposed solution to this . . . problem has

the immanent Trinity equal to the economic Trinity,[64] allegedly brought the doctrine of the Trinity more in the midst of the (Roman Catholic) Church to open the mystery of salvation for everyone. Since economically the Son shares with the Father, he relates to him in the Origenistic sense, making his humanity more relatable to people. "Jesus is not simply God in general, but the Son. The second divine person, God's Logos is man, and only he is man."[65] By deleting the divinity from Christ Jesus and localizing him in history makes him more approachable.

Wolfhart Pannenberg, 1928–2014 AD, another inventive voice, to rouse interest in the trinitarian doctrine, summed up the intra-trinitarian relations with an eschatological direction.[66] "Relations among the three persons that are defined as mutual self-distinction cannot be reduced to relations of origin in the traditional sense. The Father does not merely beget the Son. He also hands over his kingdom to him and receives it back from him. The Son is not merely begotten of the Father. He is also obedient to him and he thereby glorifies him as the one God. The Spirit is not just breathed. He also fills the Son and glorifies him in his obedience to the Father, thereby glorifying the Father himself. In so doing he leads into all truth (John 16:13) and searches out the deep things of God (1 Cor. 2:10–11)."[67] This scheme appeals to an eschatological push, proleptically. "Revelation is not comprehended completely in the beginning, but at the end of the

---

become famous, and axiomatic for virtually all recent Trinitarian theorizing, under the name 'Rahner's rule': 'The 'economic' Trinity is the 'immanent' Trinity and the 'immanent' Trinity is the 'economic Trinity.'"

Anatolios. *Retrieving Nicaea*, 4, "Rahner's axiom seems to strictly conflate God's eternal trinitarian being with the economic features acquired by the Trinity in God's work of salvation."

64. I find transcendent-immanent structuring more revealing than immanent-economic configuration; the former rather than the latter envisions the distance between the Trinity and his revelation in the created order.

65. Rahner. *The Trinity*, 23.

66. Holmes. *The Quest for the Trinity*, 17, "God's Lordship will be unambiguously actual in the End, but before the End there is an ambiguity about it, and it is not just that we do not clearly see God as Lord of all creation, but that the fact of God's Lordship remain provisional until it is finally demonstrated to have always been the case in the End, although it is anticipated in the coming of Jesus, itself an anticipation of the eschaton."

Braaten. *Christ and Counter-Christ*, 45, "Pannenberg fears that faith becomes arbitrary and self-deluding if its contents are relegated to an 'invulnerable area' in which no rational methods of verification can be applied."

67. Pannenberg. *Systematic Theology*, I, 320.

revealing history."[68] By prolepsis,[69] the Church grasping the coming future, Pannenberg too sought to make the biblical trinitarian teaching more relevant in and to the Church.

Paul Tillich, AD 1886-1965, amidst surging 20th-century trinitarian interests, minimized and disparaged the Trinity's significance. "The doctrine of the Trinity does not affirm the logical nonsense that three is one and one is three; it describes in dialectical terms the inner movement of the divine life as an eternal separation from itself and return to itself. Theology is not expected to accept a senseless combination of words, that is, genuine logical thinking. Dialectical thinking is not in conflict with structure of thinking."[70] Throughout, he hung onto and worked theologically with Renaissance-Enlightenment-Modernism secularization. This disapproving spirit he reflected at the end of his *Systematic Theology*. "Like every theological symbol, the trinitarian symbolism must be understood as an answer to the questions implied in man's predicament. It is the most inclusive answer and rightly has the dignity attributed to it in the liturgical practice of the church. Man's predicament, out of which the existential questions arise, must be characterized by three concepts: finitude with respect to man's essential being as creature, estrangement with respect to man's existential being in time and space, ambiguity with respect to man's participation in life universal."[71] Non-participating in the rise of trinitarian reflections, however eclectic and erroneous, set Tillich off from 20th-century theological scholars.

Jurgen Moltmann, AD 1926-2024, in his social doctrine of the Trinity, found that the Three, without hierarchy, always existed in the *perichoresis* (interpenetrative) mode in which God the Father also suffers.[72] This interpenetration and suffering, future oriented, occurs in Scriptures' eschatological bedding.

---

68. Pannenberg, "Dogmatic Theses on the Doctrine of Revelation," 123-55, in Pannenberg, ed., *Revelation As History*, 131.

69. Prolepsis: reading the future into the present.

70. Tillich. *Systemic Theology, I*, 56.

71. Tillich. *Systematic Theology, III*, 285-86.

72. Holmes. *The Quest for the Trinity*, 21, ". . . he develops an avowedly 'social' doctrine of the Trinity: three persons, mutually interrelated, mutually constitutive, with no hierarchy.

Bauckham, Richard, "Jurgen Moltmann," 111-31, in Toon and Spiceland. *One God in Trinity*, 114, "Moltmann's thought seems to demand the recognition of an element of genuine becoming in God, since only this will guarantee the biblical perception that truth is to be found in event, in history and eschatology, rather than in the eternal being of the Greeks which empties the temporal process of significance."

> The eschatological is not one element *of* Christianity, but it is the medium of Christian faith as such, the key in which everything in it is set . . . The God spoken of here is not intra-worldly or extra-worldly, but the "God of hope" (Rom. 15:13),[73] a God with "future as his essential nature". . . as made known in Exodus and in Israelite prophecy, the God whom we therefore cannot really have in us or over us but always only before us, who encounters us in his promises for the future, and whom we therefore cannot "have" either, but can only await in active hope. A proper theology would therefore have to be constructed in the light of its future goal. Eschatology should not be its end, but its beginning.[74]

With this unbiblical reference to God the Father, Moltmann's theological construction worked the Trinity out as a community of Father, Son, and Spirit unified in mutual interpenetration modeled on a democratic community of free people. "This means that Christian theology is essentially compelled to perceive God himself in the passion of Christ, and to discover the passion of Christ in God."[75] Such eschatology apparently demands a genuine becoming in God the Father.

> The love with which God creatively and sufferingly loves the world is no different from the love he himself is in eternity. And conversely, creative and suffering love has always been a part of his love's eternal nature.[76]

God the Father's suffering has no foundation in Scriptures; it serves Moltmann's ideal[77] to make the Father identify with unparalleled suffering in the world.[78]

---

73. Romans 15:13, referring to Isaiah 11:10, 52:15, points to the Christ, not God the Father.

74. Moltmann. *Theology of Hope*, 16.

75. Moltmann. *The Trinity and the Kingdom: The Doctrine of God*, 22.
Toon and Spiceland. *One God in Trinity*, 113, ". . . the trinitarian truth of God is not given as the disclosure of supra-temporal truth; it is the truth of Jesus Christ who still awaits his future, of the Spirit which is the power of the resurrection of the dead, and of God who still waits to be 'all in all.'"

76. Moltmann. *The Trinity and the Kingdom: The Doctrine of God*, 59.

77. Moltmann. *The Trinity and the Kingdom: The Doctrine of God*, viii, ". . . I have developed a *social doctrine of the Trinity*, according to which God is a community of Father, Son and Spirit, whose unity is constituted by mutual indwelling and reciprocal interpeneration."

78. A biblical case may be made for God the Father's compassion in his approach to Moses as recorded in Exodus 3.
Barrett. *Simply Trinity*, 79, "Notice what word social trinitarians like Moltmann use to define the Trinity: *community. The Trinity is a community* or *society,* a cooperation of

John Zizioulas, AD 1931–2023, developed the social analogy ideal of the Cappadocian Three[79] (Basil of Caesarea, AD 330–379, Gregory of Nyssa, AD 335–95, and Gregory of Nazianzus, AD 329–89); they found in the Trinity that they connected being no longer with the substance of things but with the relationship necessary in personhood. This now redefined *hypostasis* into freedom connected with relational links.[80]

> ... when we say that God "is," we do not bind the personal freedom of God—the being of God is not an ontological "necessity" or a simple "reality" for God—but we ascribe the being of God to his personal freedom. In a more analytical way this means that God, as Father and not as substance, perpetually confirms through "being" His *free* will to exist. And it is precisely His trinitarian existence that constitutes this confirmation: the Father out of love—that is, freely—begets the Son and brings forth the Spirit. If God exists, He exists because the Father exists, that is, He who out of love freely begets the Son and brings forth the Spirit. Thus God as person—as the hypostasis of the Father—makes the one divine substance to be that which it is: the one God.[81]

Zizioulas recognized God the Father in the Origenistic sense as the source or cause of the Trinity. This ontology of the Trinity the Father grounded in freedom. As the Father freely created the Son and the Spirit, he created the universe; in that creation, the emphasis fell not on the substance of things but on the relation of the Father to the substance of the created order.

> The survival of a personal identity is possible for God not on account of His substance but on account of His trinitarian existence. If God the Father is immortal, it is because His unique and unrepeatable identity as Father is distinguished eternally from that of the Son and of the Spirit, who call Him "Father."[82]

---

divine persons, each with his own center of consciousness and will."

79. Holmes. *The Quest for the Trinity*, 12, "Zizioulas argues ... that the Cappadocian fathers developed a novel ontology, which connected being with personhood and relationship."

80. Olson and Hall. *Guides to Theology: The Trinity*, 113, "Zizioulas's favorite phrase for ultimate reality is 'ecclesial being' or 'ecclesial identity,' and he asserts that 'ecclesial being is bound to the very being of God,' that God's being is an 'event of communion.'"

81. Zizioulas. *Being as Communion*, 41, "In a more analytical way this means that God, as Father and not as substance, perpetually confirms through 'being' His *free* will to exist. And it is precisely His trinitarian existence that constitutes this confirmation: the Father out of love—that is, freely—begets the Son and brings forth the Spirit."

82. Zizioulas. *Being as Communion*, 48.

This shift from the Origenistic equality and equity of the Three-of-the-Trinity into the sovereignty of the Father with the subordination of the Son and Spirit severed the Divinity from the Scriptures.

In sum,[83] the 20th-century revival in the doctrine of the Trinity, neo-trinitarianism, disappeared in disparate directions, away from the Scriptures. These eclectic disappointments at relevancy for the Trinity resulted in lording it over the Scriptures. Whatever eisegetical effigies of godness arrived at, covetousness wraps the biblical trinitarian teaching into pseudo-deities, making the worst neighborhoods and world communities.

However much extra-biblical thinkers from within or without exert pressures to domesticate the Trinity, maximally even, to make the Divinity conform to shifting-sand ingenuities and bend the Trinity into social programming, the cultivators of these fantasies too shall kneel before the Judge of all the earth; in that moment on the border of heaven and hell, unrepentant sinners shall see only momentarily the magnificence and holiness of the Trinity, then drop away, memory intact, into the paining darkness of unending remorse. The import and impact of Philippians 2:9—11 forcefully and eternally impugns the damned. In time, all who malign the biblically trinitarian revelation shall with respective false doctrines suffer the divine wrath for now held in abeyance, while believing remnants humbly bow before the Divinity, blessing him forever and ever.

---

83. These predominantly Eurocentric neo-trinitarian illustrations oversimplify the tremendously involved and intertwined literature of many more participants; each of the above illustrations beams a light into intricacies of this neo-trinitarianism.

BIBLIOGRAPHY

Anatolios, Khalid. *Retrieving Nicaea: The Development and Meaning of Trinitarian Doctrine*, Grand Rapids: Baker Academic, 2011.

Argyle, A.W. *Knowing Christianity: God in the New Testament*, London: Hodder and Stoughton, 1965.

Augustine. *A Select Library of the Nicene and Post-Nicene Fathers of the Christian Church*. III, ed. Philip Schaff, Grand Rapids: Eerdmans, 1956.

Barrett, Matthew. *Simply Trinity: The Unmanipulated Father, Son, and Spirit*, Grand Rapids: BakerBooks, 2021.

Barth, Karl. *The Doctrine of the Word of God*, 1/1, tr. G.T. Thomson, London: T&T Clark, 1936/1969.

Berkhof, L. *Systematic Theology*, Grand Rapids: Eerdmans, 1939/1968.

Braaten, Carl E. *Christ and Counter-Christ: Apocalyptic Themes in Theology and Culture*, Philadelphia: Fortress, 1972.

Calvin, John. *The Library of Christian Classics: XX, Institutes of the Christian Religion*, ed. John T. McNeill, tr. Ford Lewis Battles, Philadelphia; Westminster, MCMLX.

Frame, John M. *A History of Western Philosophy and Theology*, Phillipsburg: Presbyterian & Reformed, 2015.

Haidt, Jonathan. *The Anxious Generation: How the Great Rewiring of Childhood Is Causing an Epidemic of Mental Illness*, New York: PenguinRandom, 2024.

Heather, Peter. *Christendom: The Triumph of a Religion, AD 300–1300*. New York: Alfred A. Knopf, 2023.

Hendriksen. W. *More Than Conquerors: An Interpretation of the Book of Revelation*, Grand Rapids, Baker, 1939, 1971.

Holmes, Stephen R. *The Quest for the Trinity: the Doctrine of God in Scripture, History and Modernity*, Downers Grove: IVP Academic, 2012.

Hoogsteen, T. *Covenant Essays: Two*, Eugene, Oregon: Resource Publications, 2022.

McDonald, Marci. *The Armageddon Factor: The Rise of Christian Nationalism in Canada*, Toronto: Random House, 2010.

Moltmann, Jurgen. *Theology of Hope: On the Ground and Implication of a Christian Eschatology*, tr. J.W. Veitch, London: SCM, 1967.

———. *The Trinity and the Kingdom: The Doctrine of God*, tr. Margaret Kohl, Minneapolis: Fortress, 1993.

Norris Jr., Richard A. *Sources of Early Christian Thought: The Christological Controversy*, ed. William G. Rush, Fortress, 1980.

Olson, Roger E. and Christopher A. Hall. *Guides to Theology: The Trinity*, Grand Rapids: Eerdmans, 2002.

Pannenberg, Wolfhart. *Systematic Theology*, I, tr. Geoffry W. Bromiley, Grand Rapids: Eerdmans, 1988.

———, ed. *Revelation as History*, tr. David Granskou, London: The Macmillan Company, 1969.

Poythress, Vern S. *The Mystery of the Trinity: A Trinitarian Approach to the Attributes of God*, Phillipsburg, Presbyterian & Reformed, 2020.

Owen, John. *The Holy Spirit: His Gifts and Powers*, Grand Rapids: Kregel, 1954, 1967.

Rahner, Karl. *Milestones in Catholic Theology: The Trinity*, New York: Herder and Herder/The Crossroad, 1967/1970.

Rhodes, Ron. *Christ Before the Manger: the life and times of the preincarnate Christ*, Eugene, Oregon: Wipf and Stock, 1992.

Rush, William G. *Sources of Early Christian Thought: The Trinitarian Controversy*, ed. William G. Rush, Fortress, 1980.

Seitz, Christopher R. *Nicene Christianity: The Future for a New Ecumenism*, Grand Rapids, Brazos, 2001.

Smith, James R. *The Forgotten Trinity: Recovering the Heart of Christian Belief*, Minneapolis, Bethany House, 1998.

Toon, Peter and James D. Spiceland, eds. *One God in Trinity: An analysis of the primary dogma of Christianity*, Westchester, IL. Cornerstone, 1980.

Tillich, Paul. *Systematic Theology, III*, Chicago, University of Chicago Press, 1967.

Weber, Otto. *Karl Barth's Church Dogmatics: An Introductory Report on Volumes I:1 to III:4*, tr. Arthur C. Cochrane, Philadelphia: Westminster, 1953.

White, James R. *The Forgotten Trinity: Recovering the Heart of Christian Belief*, Minneapolis: Bethany House, 2019.

Zizioulas, John D. *Being as Communion: Studies in Personhood and the Church*, St Vladimir's Seminary, New York, 1985.

www.ingramcontent.com/pod-product-compliance
Lightning Source LLC
Chambersburg PA
CBHW071430160426
43195CB00013B/1857